MILLENNIAL
VEGAN

MILLENNIAL
VEGAN

Tips for Navigating Relationships, Wellness,
and Everyday Life as a Young Animal Advocate

Casey T. Taft, PhD

2017

Danvers

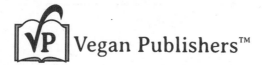 Vegan Publishers™

Vegan Publishers
Danvers, Massachusetts
www.veganpublishers.com

Cover and text design by Nicola May Design

ISBN: 978-1-940184-40-1

Contents

Preface: You Are Awesome

> " I just want all of the animal rights activists to know that you are doing a great thing for the planet! I know how it feels to fight for the animals and to question what your life means. I know how it feels to get teased, bullied, and ridiculed for wanting to help animals. I have so much love and respect for all of you, and you are saving so many lives! "

> " I'm really proud of my daughter. She has decided to go vegan because she learned about the cruelty behind the animal use industries from social media. Many of her friends and even her professors are not kind to her when it comes to her veganism, but she's been vegan for almost a year now and she says she's never going back. She told me how much my support means to her, and our relationship is better than it's ever been. I tell her that I think she's amazing just about every day for sticking with her convictions. "

I want to start by stating the obvious: you are awesome. I sincerely mean that and this is why I think it's so important to support your efforts. I want to provide you with whatever tools and tips might be useful to you, because you have selflessly and courageously stood up for nonhuman animals, and I want you to know that I applaud and stand up for you.

A recent survey[1] in the United Kingdom showed that approximately 42 percent of all vegans can be considered "Millennials," falling between the ages of 15 and 34 years old, compared to just 14 percent who are over age 65. This younger generation is increasingly able to see past all of the ways that our society indoctrinates us to use nonhuman animals. What makes this even more impressive is that they are doing so despite being screwed over economically by prior generations. More Millennials have received a college degree than any prior generation, and yet they are carrying the most debt ever and are struggling to find decent jobs.[2]

Animal use and abuse is all around us and is taught to us from the time we are born, and it is present in all of society's institutions. I wasn't quite aware of just how ubiquitous it was until my wife and I had a child of our own. We received a lot of hand-me-down toys and books, and so many of them contained messages promoting "happy farms" and other forms of animal use. It was present in almost all of the children's programming on television and online, and we found it impossible to shield our child from it despite all of our awareness about the issue.

Of course, it goes much deeper than that. For most of us, our parents taught us that we can't be healthy without eating animals and their secretions. We were taught to love some animals, like dogs and cats; and to eat other animals, like cows, chickens, and fish. We didn't necessarily even know we were eating animals until we had been doing it long enough to question it. We were taken to zoos, animal parks, and aquariums that were considered wholesome family activities. Our clothes were often derived from nonhuman animals and we were raised to not even consider the implications of unnecessarily using the skin and fur of animals for various purposes.

As we got older and were bombarded with media images that treated animal use and killing as a fact of life, most of us were not well equipped enough to challenge it because we had been raised to accept it from birth. By that point our indoctrination into animal abuse was well rooted and difficult to see through. For most, including very intelligent and otherwise insightful and kind people, this indoctrination is never reversed.

I would love to be able to say that I was able to see through the indoctrination from a young age, like you, but I wasn't. However, there was always a part of me that found eating animals repulsive on some level. I remember forcing myself to eat them and had a hard time doing so at times when I was a child, but that repulsion was short-lived. I also remember not being able to watch my mother prepare the turkey carcass for Thanksgiving, or I wouldn't be able to eat it. So I purposely avoided any reminder that I was eating a dead animal. Because it's harder to avoid being fully aware that "seafood" is dead animals, I have never been able to eat sea creatures at all—except for one time when I had a taste of a dead lobster my father was eating, and I was disgusted.

When I was in my early twenties and still very much a non-vegan, I briefly dated an animal rights activist. She would begin to tell me about how animals are used and killed (information on this topic was not widely disseminated back then without social media), and I would tell her that I didn't want to know. I knew that it was horrible, and I didn't want to be reminded of it, knowing that if I really knew the full truth and let it truly sink in I would have to go vegan. At the time, I was struggling with various personal issues and just didn't feel like I was able to make a significant life change like that. I often wonder what the animal rights activist was thinking at the time and what she'd say now if she knew I was a vegan advocate.

The truth of the matter is that I didn't go plant-based until I was around thirty, and didn't truly go vegan until I was past my mid-thirties, despite the fact that I had a career as a psychologist developing violence prevention programs. I hadn't yet made that connection between violence toward human and nonhuman animals, despite the fact that it was looking me directly in the face. How I wish I had the clarity to recognize the gross injustice of our animal use at an earlier age.

But you were able to see past all of the indoctrination and distractions while still young, which is incredibly impressive. While most young people are struggling with issues related to self-esteem, relationships with family and peers, and dealing with the stressors of school and work, you were able to think beyond yourself to the massive suffering that nonhuman animals experience. You have already learned a lesson that has taken so many of us much longer to learn and that most people have never learned: there is no need to use nonhuman animals for any purpose, and therefore it can't be ethical to do so.

When we live a life that is consistent with our moral values, we have more meaning and can effect great change. When we think of the well-being and safety of those other than ourselves, we have the opportunity to lead a more rewarding life. As a psychologist I have learned that one of the best ways to treat depression and other issues is through helping others. Therefore you have gotten your life started on the right foot. People like you provide me with hope for the future of the survival of this planet and all who inhabit it. No pressure, though!

Having more awareness than others around you comes with a great cost as well, unfortunately, and that's why I have written this book. I have heard from so many of you who are being bullied by your peers, or worse yet, family and friends. If you're not being bullied, perhaps you're struggling with the fact that your loved ones don't seem to understand your veganism and are not supportive. It's hard enough for an adult to not receive that support, but many young people are reliant on their families for many things, such as food shopping, so it can be extra challenging. Or perhaps those closest to you are really trying to understand and support you but just don't know how. It is also likely that you struggle with the knowledge of the harm that we collectively do to animals in society, while being forced to observe those you care about participating in such atrocities by funding animal industries.

Or perhaps you have a supportive network, or even come from a vegan family, and you're just trying to learn more about veganism and how to advocate for animals in the best way possible for you. This is also a focus of this book, since navigating the waters of animal advocacy is not easy, and there is a lot to learn. As a psychologist who has helped many people end needless violence, and who has recently written a book on motivational methods for vegan advocacy, I believe that I have some insight into how to best reach others with your advocacy as a young vegan.

Regardless of your specific situation, I am in awe of you and want to help. You may find some material more personally relevant than other material. My hope is that you can come away with something of value that you can apply to your life to make being vegan easier for you and to help you with your advocacy. I hope that you, like me, feel that being vegan is a joy, but I understand that there are certain challenges that you encounter as a younger vegan that I don't have to face.

This book is intended to help you better deal with social isolation, to get the support you need, to communicate with friends and family more effectively, to have information regarding some important issues like eating disorders and mental health problems, and to be the most effective animal advocate that you can be. If you feel like it might be helpful, after you've read it, I encourage you to pass this book along to the people you care about so that they can gain greater awareness about your veganism that may help set the stage for better communication.

I have found that it can sometimes be easier to provide some-body with reading material to learn on their own before having important discussions. Perhaps you will be able to have more productive conversations with loved ones once they have some basic information about veganism as well as some insight into some of the things you might be dealing with.

I have heard from so many young and aspiring vegans from my work as co-owner of Vegan Publishers and running its Facebook page. So I will illustrate some of these important topics with quotes that are adapted from interactions I've had online, like the two at the start of this preface. I have altered them so that nobody can be identifiable, but these examples are drawn from real-life people and situations. I want people to understand the seriousness of the issues that I discuss by having real quotes, stories, and conversations to illustrate them.

Acknowledgements

I want to thank all of those who stand up for others despite negative personal consequences. You have my full appreciation.

An Introduction to Veganism

> I just wanted to say thank you to all the vegans who have been so supportive. I know that our efforts may seem useless at times, but I want you to know that I appreciate you so much for working to save the lives of animals, humans, and our planet. It's a great comfort to me to know that I am not fighting this fight alone and that love will win. There is so much violence and injustice in this world, but there is hope through veganism. Thank you, friends, from the bottom of my heart.

> This is for those interested or transitioning to veganism. We're living at a time where information is at our fingertips and there is increasing support for those who want to end animal use. When we think of the animals instead of ourselves, veganism becomes a lot easier and there is no need for baby steps. If you're not vegan yet, you can and should go vegan this second, and I'd be happy to help. So take a deep breath, learn everything you can about the gross injustices animals experience, ask for information and advice, get excited about making this incredible change, and make the decision to go vegan.

What Is Veganism?

Given that what it means to be vegan is not well understood, it may be helpful to start with discussing its definition, especially since popular culture and mainstream animal advocacy organizations promote the view that veganism is simply a diet.

The concept of veganism originally put forward by the Vegan Society was about ethics and minimizing the harm we do to non-human animals in all ways that we can, and that has never changed.[1] The definition of veganism described by Leslie J. Cross in 1949 involved "the principle of the emancipation of animals from exploitation by man." The definition was later modified: "to seek an end to the use of animals by man for food, commodities, work, hunting, vivisection, and by all other uses involving exploitation of animal life by man." When the Vegan Society became a registered charity in 1979, it was further refined as follows:

> A philosophy and way of living which seeks to exclude—as far as is possible and practicable—all forms of exploitation of, and cruelty to, animals for food, clothing or any other purpose; and by extension, promotes the development and use of animal-free alter- natives for the benefit of humans, animals and the environment.

As this definition makes clear, veganism is about more than what one eats or consumes, and being vegan is not simply about going without things or restricting one's diet. To be vegan means to live life by the ethic of minimizing the suffering of other sentient beings and to make the world a better place for all. It is about rejecting injustice and embracing a respect for all forms of life and bringing an awareness of that respect to the world.

Sometimes young vegans get confused about the meaning of veganism and view it as a health thing. I've seen some vegans say that they believe that all vegans need to be thin and in great shape because we are advertising veganism to the world. That couldn't be further from the truth. Veganism is about ethics, not our bodies. While there are health benefits of veganism, vegans come in all shapes and sizes. We should not be judging anyone based on their bodies, and that kind of behavior can really keep others feeling left out of the movement, much to the detriment of the nonhuman animals we are fighting for. So please don't judge anyone based on their diets, their bodies, or your perceptions of what others should be doing to promote your version of veganism.

BENEFITS OF VEGANISM

The simplest and most powerful argument for veganism is that we have no need to contribute to animal suffering and the deaths of over one trillion nonhuman animals every year from human use of them. These animals are needlessly bred to produce massive amounts of "food," which does great damage to their bodies and leads to immense suffering. They are mistreated in unspeakable ways that are considered standard practice in various animal use industries, and they are killed after living only a tiny fraction of their natural lives, all for products that we don't need.

While veganism was relatively unheard of in the not-too-distant past, the vegan movement is rapidly gaining steam and is now entering the mainstream of American culture, though mainstream and celebrity vegans often confuse veganism with a simple dietary choice. Old views of veganism as a "fringe" or "radical" concept are fading as social media has helped to raise vegan awareness and as we also learn more about the many side benefits of veganism, such as human and environmental health.

There used to be a common sentiment that plant-based diets were unhealthy, extreme, and potentially dangerous. Such notions have now been debunked by a wealth of available medical and nutritional research data that suggests the opposite is true. Evidence indicates that a plant-based diet is associated with lower cholesterol levels and cardiovascular disease risk,[2] lower risk of dying from heart disease,[3] lower blood pressure[4] and hypertension risk,[5] lower rates of cancer,[6] and decreased risk for other problems such as cataracts,[7] dementia,[8] allergies,[9] and acne.[10] Randomized controlled trial studies, the most powerful research design possible to show the benefits of something, show that plant-based diets are effective for helping to lose weight,[11] controlling type 2 diabetes,[12] and actually reversing the progression of coronary heart disease[13] and prostate cancer.[14]

Regarding the environment, a staggering 30 percent of the earth's ice-free land mass is used for animal agriculture[15] and these animals produce more than half of all human-induced greenhouse gas emissions,[16] higher than all forms of transportation in the world combined.[17] Nearly half of the water consumed in the United States is used for "livestock,"[18] and we face the prospect of future catastrophic food shortages due to lack of water resources,[19] and "livestock" consume considerably more food resources than humans consume directly.[20] Waste from animal feedlots on farms is also a major contributor to water quality impairments and global "dead zones" in our oceans,[21] air pollution,[22] and deforestation.[23]

Myths about Veganism

> **"**
>
> I just spoke with a cardiologist who said that by promoting veganism and telling them to eat more fruits, vegetables, nuts, seeds, and legumes, I was a threat to the overall health of his patients! I'm actually in shock that he truly believes this and instead promotes something called a "wheat belly" diet, which is similar to Atkins. He's recommending that his patients load up on animal products that have been shown to increase risk for heart disease! Then, when their heart cholesterol goes through the roof and heart disease worsens, he puts stents in their arteries and sends them home on statins. I couldn't believe my ears.
>
> **"**

Common misconceptions about veganism abound, and vegans have likely heard them all countless times. As the quotation above illustrates, these myths are held even by those who are supposed to have at least some knowledge about these issues (though those in medical professions receive virtually no lessons about nutrition during their training). Here I discuss only a handful of the many misconceptions that people often have about veganism and some corrective information that may be helpful in your conversations with others. However, as I will discuss later, I think it's important that we don't get too caught up debating with others about these issues because they're not really central to the reasons for our veganism. To be vegan means to opt out of the dominant paradigm in our society that thinks of nonhuman animals as commodities. When discussions get sidetracked over various issues related to veganism, we are usually better off bringing it back to the central point that we have no need to be using animals for any purpose, and therefore it can't be ethical to needlessly use them.

"Vegans don't get enough protein"

The idea that one cannot get enough protein without consuming meat and dairy is a commonly propagated myth that vegans are frequently reminded of by well-meaning non-vegans. There are, in fact, abundant sources of protein that vegans commonly consume, including beans, soy-based products, and various other plant sources, such as seeds and nuts. It may be surprising to learn that all plants contain protein and that common vegetables are excellent sources of protein. For example, broccoli contains more than twice the protein per calorie of cow flesh, and spinach is about equal to the flesh of chicken and fish in terms of protein per calorie.

Nutritional research indicates that vegans have no difficulty meeting their dietary protein requirements assuming they consume enough calories.[24] Evidence does not suggest a benefit of consuming greater than 10 percent of calories from protein, even for athletes, and thus people typically consume much more protein than is necessary. There is actually evidence indicating that diets too rich in animal protein may be unhealthy. For example, one study of elderly women found that consumption of a high ratio of animal to vegetable protein was related to more bone loss and risk of hip fracture.[25] Another study suggested that high intake of animal protein accelerated kidney function problems in women with mild renal insufficiency.[26]

There used to be a common misconception that vegans needed to consume complementary proteins, like beans and rice, together so that foods with incomplete essential amino acid content could combine to form a complete protein.[27] More recently, however, the author of this theory as well as the larger nutrition establishment has rejected this idea based on a lack of research evidence to support it,[28] though eating a variety of protein sources is optimal.[29]

"VEGANS CAN'T GET VITAMIN B_{12} FROM NON-ANIMAL SOURCES"

Vitamin B_{12} is an essential vitamin used to synthesize red blood cells and maintain nervous system health. A B_{12} deficiency can lead to neurological problems, weakness, and fatigue. It is a myth that B_{12} is animal-based and can only be obtained by consuming meat and dairy; it is actually produced by bacteria commonly found in the soil around plants and is also found in animals that consume these microorganisms. Our human ancestors had an easier time getting B_{12} because they lived more closely with other animals and food, and water was not purified like it is today.

Another misconception about B_{12} is that vegans are at high risk for B_{12} deficiency. There is indeed evidence suggesting that vegans have lower B_{12} concentrations than non-vegans.[30] However, a lack of B_{12} consumption is very rarely the cause of a B_{12} deficiency in a normal vegan diet, with one expert estimating odds of less than one in a million.[31] The human body requires very minimal amounts of B_{12}—less than any other vitamin. Rather, a B_{12} deficiency is almost always caused by a digestive problem such as celiac disease or Crohn's disease where there is a disruption in one's ability to absorb nutrients.[32]

Some nutrition experts highlight the importance of vegans consuming adequate B_{12} to prevent milder B_{12} deficiency that leads to a rise in homocysteine, an amino acid, over the course of several years.[33] Research shows that homocysteine imbalance may be linked with cancer development, autoimmune diseases, vascular dysfunction, and neurodegenerative disease.[34] Regardless of the specific level of risk of B_{12} deficiency, vegans should ensure sufficient B_{12} levels by taking a B_{12} supplement or consuming foods enriched with B_{12}, such as soy milks, rice milks, and cereals. B_{12} supplementation is particularly important for pregnant or nursing women, because B_{12} in a woman's body is less available for the baby during this time.[35] The elderly are also at higher risk for B_{12} deficiency due to absorption problems.[36] Vegans are perhaps in an even better position than non-vegans to avoid B_{12}

deficiency because they are often more aware of the need to take B_{12} supplements, and this possible protective effect takes on greater importance in the elderly as B_{12} absorption problems become more common.[37] In other words, vegans' heightened awareness of B_{12} may serve them well, relative to non-vegans who generally do not think much about B_{12} at all.

"VEGANS HAVE NO JOY IN THEIR LIVES"

> **"**
>
> I'm sick of hearing people refer to my diet as "rabbit food" despite the fact that I love French fries, devour vegan pizza and nachos, and frequently indulge in fine dark chocolate and coconut ice cream sundaes!
>
> **"**

Most vegans will tell you that the notion that vegans do not enjoy food or other aspects of life, presumably because it involves the use of nonhuman animals, is the furthest thing from the truth. With vegan alternatives to pretty much everything nowadays, vegans don't in any way have to sacrifice their enjoyment of eating. For example, many of the vegans I know consider themselves "foodies" and make a point of exploring new vegan recipes. One notable vegan, Kristin Lajeunesse, has recently travelled throughout the United States, living out of her van and eating only at vegan restaurants to promote vegan dining and the different food options that are out there for vegans. She writes about her vegan travels on her blog, *Will Travel for Vegan Food*.[38]

I often hear from my non-vegan friends and colleagues that they could not possibly survive without meat or dairy, or that it must be very hard to be vegan. Many or most vegans will tell you that they found the transition to be much easier than they thought it would be and that they began to notice feeling better physically and even mentally or spiritually soon after making the change.

Non-vegans will often ask vegans if they "can" or "cannot" eat certain foods. As Colleen Patrick-Goudreau wrote in *Vegan's Daily Companion*:

> The people asking if I "can" eat something are not trying to be malicious; if anything, they are being considerate, and I always let them know that I appreciate they've remembered I'm vegan. But also, I don't want to miss the opportunity to offer them a different perspective about what it means to be vegan—that it is indeed about choice and not deprivation or willpower.[39]

In other words, when we are living vegan, we don't feel like we're depriving ourselves. In fact, it's really the opposite. When we live in a way that's consistent with our values, we tend to be happier and healthier. When we have developed true awareness of the harm that humans do to nonhuman animals in so many ways, opting out of contributing to this harm feels like the only course of action we can truly take that will provide us with greater peace of mind. We're focusing on preventing needless violence and injustice toward others.

"Vegans do more harm to plants than non-vegans"

> **"**
>
> Someone is actually trying to debate me by saying that vegans are just as unethical as non-vegans for eating plants because they "have feelings." I really can't. I mean I'm not going to debate hypotheticals with someone who eats animals who we know for a fact are sentient and feel pain and a range of emotions.
>
> **"**

Most vegans regularly hear jokes about how vegans kill more plants than non-vegans, suggesting that eating plants and animals are morally equivalent. While this is typically raised in a joking fashion, or in a way that attempts to get under the skin of vegans (and it does!), I have heard non-vegans seriously argue that vegans do more harm than good because they contribute to the killing of so many plants! This is factually incorrect, since the production of animal-based food leads to the use of more plants than would be needed if those plants were simply consumed directly. Regardless, the simple fact that plants do not have pain receptors or central nervous systems is usually enough to end arguments over plant "torture" and needless killing. When others begin to argue that there is "research" of plant sentience, ask them to provide a link to a single peer-reviewed scientific study that plants think and feel like animals do, rather than a headline-grabbing article found online. You will effectively end the discussion because no such scientific evidence exists.

This is not to say that we should be unconcerned about killing plants. I believe that we should do as little harm to plant life in addition to animal life. However, as vegans we are most concerned with "sentient" life, or those who have the ability to think or feel. Nobody would argue with a straight face that mowing the lawn is morally equivalent to slitting the throats of a hundred baby animals, regardless of how much one loves plants.

"GOD PUT NONHUMAN ANIMALS HERE FOR US TO EAT"

This is one of the more common justifications we hear for killing and consuming animals. People often use religion to justify some of our most horrible practices, including the needless killing of nonhuman animals. Of course, passages from the Bible and other religious texts can be taken to either justify the killing or make the case against the killing of animals, and I have witnessed several debates among those using passages from religious texts to make their arguments for or against our use of animals. This passage from *Free From Harm* cautions us not to use religious traditions or literal interpretations of religious texts to attempt to make a case against harming nonhuman animals:

> The Bible and religion in general have historically been used to justify rape, incest, infanticide, murder, war, racism, sexism, homophobia, slavery, and many other acts of violence, oppression and persecution. Does a Biblical or religious precedent make any of these actions less immoral? Of course not.
>
> Instead of citing, for example, what Jesus was said to have possibly eaten in Biblical times, it would be far more relevant to ask, *What would Jesus do today*, if he lived in the age of industrialized agriculture where billions of animals are bred through artificial insemination, treated like mere commodities and processed like worthless pieces of meat—used and killed not from necessity, but just to satisfy our taste buds and to line the pockets of wealthy industrialists?" Would he praise humankind for respecting his creations? Or would he instead invoke The Golden Rule? Would he not

insist that, when given a choice between mercy and cruelty, a Christian is compelled to choose compassion over violence?[40]

One might also question why a higher power would place nonhuman animals on this planet so many years before humans if it were their intention for animals to only serve humans. Moreover, why would animals be created to feel a range of emotions and pain if their purpose was to be killed and eaten by humans? Would a benevolent god purposely expose sentient beings to unnecessary pain and harm? These are questions for which there are no satisfactory answers.

As veganism has gained in popularity and acceptance, we have witnessed religious figures and authors who have discussed how the vegan ethic is consistent with their basic teachings. It has long been confusing to me how we can promote an ethic to minimize the harm we do to others, while at the same time consuming non-human animals every day, which necessarily contributes to their harm. There are specific movements and organizations within Eastern religions in particular, such as Buddhism, where efforts have been made to make these connections and include non-human animals in basic teachings of kindness and respect for all living beings.

"VEGANS DON'T CARE ABOUT HUMANS"

Many assume that vegans care only about nonhuman animals and don't care about humans. A 2012 blog post by Anjali Sareen on *The Huffington Post* illustrates her response to this issue:

> "You're vegan? Why do you hate people?" I get asked this question on a fairly regularly basis, and yet each time it catches me off-guard. I always have a hard time imagining a person's initial reaction to my plant-based diet and cruelty free lifestyle will

be anger and irritation. I'm never quite sure how to respond. The honest answer is that I don't hate people and actually, veganism harmonizes perfectly with a lot of very important human rights issues. My lifestyle philosophy is about uplifting the world—not, as many believe, uplifting animals at the expense of the world. [41]

Caring about humans and caring about nonhuman animals ought not be mutually exclusive. Rather, a true vegan perspective should be exactly the opposite; it should emphasize justice for *all* sentient beings. In chapter 9 I discuss the importance of moral consistency in effective animal advocacy, and in chapters 10 and 11 I discuss the dangers of developing a misanthropic advocacy perspective.

It is also important to note that forms of injustice experienced by both are inextricably linked. For example, overwhelming evidence shows that animal abuse is more prevalent in homes in which family violence occurs[42] and that cruelty to animals is a precursor to violence and criminal behavior later in life.[43] Further, as discussed in Gail Eisnitz's book, *Slaughterhouse*,[44] those who work on animal farms exhibit problems with perpetrating violence in their personal lives and suffer from a range of mental health issues. Thus, it is not a great leap of logic to suggest that minimizing violence toward nonhuman animals should assist in reducing violence directed toward humans.

There has been increasing recognition of intersections between different forms of oppression that include animal use.[45] Intersectionality, or the study of overlapping social identities and recognition of systems of oppression that are connected and share common root causes,[46] has been expanded by activists to connect human and nonhuman oppression.[47] A pro-intersectional view recognizes that the root of speciesism, racism, sexism, ableism, ageism, homo- and trans-antagonism, and other "isms" is the notion that some individuals are "lesser" than others. We should help others recognize that none of us are any "higher," "better," or "more deserving" than any other, and counter injustice in all its forms.

The recognition of intersections between different forms of injustice by so many young vegans gives me hope that we are moving in the right direction toward tackling the seemingly insurmountable problems that we face as a society. Only when we collectively challenge all oppression will we see progress toward a more just world. It simply makes no sense, and is indeed speciesist, to only care about injustice toward one species of animal, be it human or nonhuman. We should speak out for all of those who experience oppression and injustice.

"Veganism is wrong because humans are naturally carnivorous"

The argument that humans are natural meat-eaters is perhaps the most common argument that I hear against veganism. Some will argue that eating animal "products" is in our DNA as humans. By and large, most of us grew up with the idea that some animals were put on Earth for us to eat, so it is natural to think that humans have always been big animal consumers.

The truth is that it does not actually matter, and debates about whether humans are "natural" flesh-eaters are unproductive. What humans ate millions of years ago really is not relevant for the food choices we make today. What matters most is the present and the ethics of our food choices given our current available food supply, food production methods, and dietary needs, which are very different from those of primitive humans. We should always bring the discussion back to the fact that we have no need to be consuming animals in this day and age, given our food options. However, it is worth having an understanding of the actual scientific evidence, which suggests that human are not at all biologically or evolutionarily predisposed to eat large amounts of meat.

Dr. Milton Mills, Associate Director of Preventive Medicine for the Physicians Committee for Responsible Medicine (PCRM), provided an interesting comparative analysis of how humans compare to carnivores and herbivores with respect to several components of anatomy.[48] For example, he discussed how carnivorous animals have a wide mouth opening in relation to their head size, a massive temporalis muscle to chew other animals, limited lower jaw movement, blade-shaped cheek molars, teeth spaced far apart, prong-like incisors, and long dagger-like canines used to stab, tear, and kill other animals. The saliva of carnivores does not contain digestive enzymes, and they bite off large chunks of animal meat and swallow them whole.

Herbivores, on the other hand, have well-developed facial musculature, fleshy lips, a smaller oral cavity, and a thicker, more muscular tongue to push plant-based food back and forth to disrupt plant cell walls to increase digestibility and allow for digestive enzymes in saliva to assist this process. Herbivores also have a jaw joint that is positioned above the plane of the teeth to better chew plants, a smaller temporalis muscle, a lower jaw that has a pronounced sideways motion when chewing to grind up plants, molars that are square and flattened, incisors that are broad and flattened, and canines that are relatively small.

In short, humans share all of these described features of herbivores and none of carnivores. Mills similarly described how humans' stomach type and acidity level, internal organs (small intestine, colon, liver, kidneys), and nails are all consistent with herbivores and not carnivores. For example, carnivores' stomachs are twenty times more acidic than herbivores' and humans' stomachs to assist in digesting other animals, and carnivores have much smaller and smoother intestinal tracts than herbivores and humans so that meat can pass through easily. Herbivores and humans have bumpier intestines to allow for plant food to move slowly to assist digestion.

Herbivores also lack the claws possessed by carnivorous animals for killing their prey. Carnivorous animals do not need to cook their meat to digest it and avoid disease; they eat entire animals and do not suffer from heart disease (only humans experience heart disease), lactose intolerance, or dairy allergies. Carnivores are also thrilled by the chase and killing of their prey and find eating raw meat pleasurable. Most humans, on the other hand, generally do not find the direct killing of animals to be pleasurable in the slightest, particularly for the consumption of the animal's raw flesh. As Pythagoras once argued, "If you declare that you are naturally designed for such a diet, then first kill for yourself what you want to eat. Do it, however, only through your own resources, unaided by cleaver or cudgel or any kind of ax."

Some argue that a lack of Vitamin B_{12} in a vegan diet is evidence that humans are naturally carnivorous. As previously discussed, however, B_{12} is produced by bacteria found in the soil and is not found solely in meat, and earlier humans likely had many more sources for obtaining B_{12} than modern humans have.

It is commonly thought that early humans hunted and ate meat, but the existing scientific evidence suggests that this only occurred in recent human history, according to Drs. Donna Hart and Robert Sussman, anthropologists who received the 2006 W.W. Howells Book Prize for *Man the Hunted: Primates, Predators, and Human Evolution.*[49] This compelling book uses fossil evidence and observations of other primates to argue that early humans fell victim to a wide variety of predators for millions of years, and that the human brain and human intelligence grew and developed as an adaptation in order to learn to outsmart predators over the course of approximately seven to ten million years.

As Hart and Sussman discuss, many fossils of the earliest humans demonstrate evidence of humans being prey to a variety of predators (e.g., puncture marks from saber-toothed cat fangs and claw marks from raptors). Examination of fossil evidence dating back nearly seven million years also indicates that Australopithecus afarensis, an early human species, was not dentally adapted to eat animals, as we have described is the case with modern humans. Further, the first modern tools to kill animals did not appear until nearly two million years ago and the first evidence of the domestication of fire that would be necessary to cook animals is from about 400 thousand years ago. The authors related their findings to modern humans by stating that "we humans are not slaughter-prone assassins by nature. We often act badly, maliciously, cruelly, but that is by choice and not by our status as bipedal primates."

"Vegan diets are expensive"

Some argue that they cannot change to a vegan diet because they think it is too expensive. While it is true that in some geographical areas known for "food deserts" affordable fruits and vegetables are harder to come by, most vegans find a vegan diet to actually be more affordable than their previous non-vegan diet. Commonly consumed vegan foods such as beans, tofu, tempeh, fruits, vegetables, and nuts tend to be cheaper than most animal-based foods. Vegan options when dining out also tend to be less expensive than non-vegan options. One great resource for eating vegan on a budget is the book *Eat Vegan on $4 a Day*.[50]

"Vegans are angry and push their agenda on others"

> "
> One of my Facebook friends just called me an angry, self-centered, judgmental wanker simply for standing up for what I believe in. Haters gonna hate, I guess. This only makes me stronger in my resolve to speak out for animals!
> "

This is sort of a combination of two myths that I'd like to discuss together. First, the notion that vegans are somehow angrier than non-vegans and therefore their views are somehow less valid is a strategy that's been used to counter other social justice movements. Stereotypes such as the "angry feminist" and the "angry black man" have commonly been used in an attempt to silence women and anti-racists.

I don't believe that vegans are angrier than the general population. In fact, I believe it's quite the opposite. Vegans are by definition peace loving and devoted to minimizing violence and harm to others. That said, vegans have every reason to feel angry, and I will never tell a vegan that they shouldn't be angry about the needless violence people inflict on nonhuman animals. As I discuss in later chapters, how we communicate that anger is what's most important. It's normal and natural to feel anger when faced with such injustice, but certain ways of expressing that anger are more effective and productive than others.

As I discuss in chapter 3, advocating for animals in a clear and assertive way should always be our goal because that is the most effective communication strategy that allows us to be heard. And assertive advocacy is not "pushing an agenda" for our personal gain; it is about the animals. We don't advocate for animals for us; it's for them. And we are not pushing anything by speaking out for animals. We are trying to raise awareness and help others see what we see. We don't accuse those who fight against our societal domestic violence problem of somehow pushing an anti–domestic violence perspective. Nor should anyone attempt to shame an animal advocate for advocating for animals. If anybody is pushing an agenda on others, it's those who consume animal "products" and force animals to die to suit their taste buds or other trivial wants.

It's Lonely Being Vegan

> When I posted on my Facebook page that zoos are unethical prisons for animals, my mother commented, "Without zoos, how would children develop an appreciation for all of these different animals?" This was just after we had a family vacation where I had to watch them all eat animal corpses for every meal the entire week. How's that for animal appreciation? For the first time since I really became aware and went vegan, I'm feeling completely hopeless and alone. I have over one thousand Facebook friends who are vegan and I get a handful of likes for my vegan posts but also a lot of negative comments. I could really use some vegan support right now to help me get past this lonely feeling today.

> Lately, I've been feeling really sad and down about the world in general. I'm upset about that gorilla who was killed in that zoo, and that all of these people claim to care about animals when they eat them at pretty much every meal. I just feel so incredibly sad and don't know how to deal with it. I want to do more to help animals in zoos, those raised for slaughter, those in abused homes, and so forth, but know that there's only so much one person can do.

I constantly see these kinds of sentiments posted online from young vegans. Social justice–minded young people already have to deal with feeling like outcasts because their loved ones and most of their peers are not particularly concerned with the plight of nonhuman animals. The young vegan may not only be alienated from her peer group overall, but even those who are more progressive-minded! They may be the only "outed" vegan in their peer group. While young people may already struggle with trying to fit in, being vegan can at times feel like a social liability and they can feel completely isolated from non-vegans who don't share their same passion to prevent harm to animals.

Feelings of loneliness and isolation may also occur because when one goes vegan, their relationships may be negatively impacted or they may lose relationships entirely. When we tell others about veganism, no matter how kind we are in our presentation, sometimes it brings up a strong response. They may somehow feel shamed even when we said nothing shaming. This occurs because the mere presence of a vegan person may make one more aware of their own contribution to the suffering of animals.

This is not a phenomenon that is limited to young people. On countless occasions, I have received very defensive responses from others when I have mentioned that I'm vegan. It's a regular occurrence for non-vegans to tell vegans to "get off your high horse" or to suggest that vegans "think they're better than others," even when the vegan said no such thing and was not aggressive in any way.

As a psychologist, I recognize that these kinds of reactions stem from experiences of feeling guilt and shame. When one feels guilty for doing harm to animals, they often display a shame response that involves aggression directed toward the vegan. Rather than thinking about the root cause of their feelings of guilt and shame, they direct those negative feelings outwards to the person who is reminding them of the abuse they are contributing to.

There is not much that we as vegans can do about the negative reactions others may have from learning that we are vegan. As I will discuss later, we can make sure that our animal advocacy is non-aggressive so that we are less likely to elicit these kinds of shame responses, but that will not necessarily solve this problem. The truth is that those who feel guilt and shame in the presence of a vegan ultimately need to "own" their own feelings and to try to reconcile them in some way to feel greater peace, hopefully by going vegan. But we are not responsible for their discomfort and anger about our veganism.

One can imagine how these kinds of responses and reactions can impact the relationships of young vegans. The effects can truly be devastating. Responses may range from discomfort in the presence of the vegan to extreme bullying and abusive behavior, a topic that I will discuss in the next chapter.

It is one thing for one's friends and acquaintances to view them differently, and another for close family members to do the same, especially when they are living under their roof. Oftentimes issues related to going vegan can strain close family relationships and even do damage that threatens to be long term. Family members who were once close may be dealing with the fact that the young vegan now has closely held beliefs that run directly counter to some of the beliefs and behaviors of themselves.

For an example, I heard from a young woman who recently went vegan because of her recognition of the extreme torture and abuse that nonhuman animals experience from the animal agriculture industry. Her family, on the other hand, comes from a long line of "animal farmers," and her father still engages in these practices. Needless to say, this woman's family is not very receptive to her going vegan. Considering that she lives in their home and is dependent on them for buying her food, there is constant tension in the home around the use of animals. Her family does not believe it is healthy for her to be vegan physically or emotionally, which helps to create an environment with a great deal of conflict because veganism is now very much an important part of her identity.

Of course, the social isolation works in both directions. It's not only that certain friends and family members may distance themselves from the vegan; the vegan may do the same. When one begins to see all of the animal abuse and exploitation that's all around them, they may be inclined to do what they can to insulate themselves from this trauma exposure as much as they can. This may mean trying to find their own vegan community and engaging in less social contact with non-vegans.

Perhaps the most difficult part about being vegan is witnessing one's loved ones participating in doing harm to non-human animals despite our efforts to make them aware of this harm. Sitting down to a meal with a parent whom we love and respect, whom we have always viewed as kind and ethical, and watching them eat the corpse of a sentient animal can be very upsetting. We vegans must learn to come to grips with the fact that those around us will not necessarily become more aware of animal harm on our schedule, and they will continue to harm animals in our presence because they have yet to be deconditioned from contributing to animal use.

This is not an easy thing to accept, and I would never suggest that we should accept animal abuse. But what is a young vegan to do when they may not have any sources of support and who otherwise might have had a close relationship with family and other loved ones? How can she find a way to navigate these difficult waters when veganism is at the core of her values system and the people she cares most about rejects that?

I wish there was an easy answer to this question, and it is frankly an issue that I, myself, as a trained psychologist considered an expert in communication, have struggled with. For many of us, this is not necessarily going to be a smooth process, and perhaps recognition of this difficulty should be our first step in figuring out how to cope. If we keep the expectations for talking about veganism realistic and not overly optimistic, we may be less disappointed when we inevitably encounter difficulty.

What I have found most helpful is to always try to think of others as "pre-vegans." That is, I expect that those around me will eventually go vegan. I truly do believe that eventually, veganism will become the norm, as society becomes more aware of the injustice of animal use via social media and other forms of vegan education, and the devastating environmental and economic impacts of animal use become too difficult to ignore any longer.

My thinking that others will eventually go vegan on a different timeline than me helps me to have a more optimistic and charitable view toward them. I recognize that I haven't always been vegan myself, and I'm glad that others didn't shut me out of their lives previously because I contributed to the harm of nonhuman animals. I eventually saw the light, but it was long after I first heard about the horrors of animal use. If I can think of others in that same way, it will be easier for me to accept them into my life, and I will be far more likely to be able to reach them with a vegan message when they are ready to receive my message.

I have found that the most difficult time for vegans interpersonally is when they first go vegan. When one goes vegan they are typically still learning about veganism—learning about the ethical side of things, nutrition, and various other topics such as human anatomy and evolutionary history because these invariably become topics of discussion surrounding veganism. It's difficult to still be in the process of learning about veganism while also feeling the need to defend veganism and help nonhuman animals. We may not necessarily have all of the facts and arguments at our disposal when we first go vegan, which can heighten the frustration level and risk for arguments with others.

When one has been vegan for a longer period of time, our veganism is just a part of who we are, and we are better able to discuss the ethics of using animals and related topics because we have had such discussions many times before. We will typically be less emotionally and physiologically charged when having these discussions as we become more and more confident and clear in our views. Eventually, there will be no justification for harming animals that we can't easily dismiss with simple ethical reasoning, logic, and science, and that makes it much easier to have calmer discussions.

Good communication and emotional expression is key for maintaining positive relationships with loved ones when we go vegan, as I will be discussing in later chapters. The better we are able to clearly and unapologetically let others know about how we feel about our veganism and associated interpersonal issues, the more likely we will be to not only facilitate a better understanding among whomever we're communicating with, but they will also better be able to see the moral imperative of veganism.

Not all families and relationships will suffer when we go vegan. I have encountered many families supportive of their vegan family member and many friends and loved ones who have attempted to better understand vegans, and I've also seen many of these folks go vegan themselves! I must say that I'm truly jealous of those vegans who were able to convince their entire families to go vegan, and can imagine how cool that must be.

At the other extreme, I've observed many relationships dissolve and end following one's transition to veganism. In some cases, bullying and abusive behavior toward the vegan is a major problem, which will be discussed in a later chapter. I certainly would not recommend a one-size-fits-all approach for young vegans in managing these issues, because every situation and every person is different. It is a sad fact that some relationships are best terminated if that ultimately means that the individual will be happier and healthier as a result. I discuss issues related to setting limits focused on using assertiveness skills in the next chapter.

Regardless of your exact social and family situation, I hope that you never waiver in your veganism and that your veganism gives you confidence that you're doing something positive for others and for the planet. Your relationships don't define you, and you should feel good about yourself knowing that you're doing your part to prevent and reduce violence in this world. You are a strong and confident person and have the power of your convictions, and you should feel proud of yourself.

Finally, keep in mind that you help to create your own social world. If you feel lonely and want to interact with more like-minded people, perhaps you can start a vegan club at school or online. You can get involved with local or national animal advocacy groups or go to events in your community. There are almost always at least some "animal people" in the local area with whom you might find some kind of connection, and you can find an animal advocate who may help mentor you. If there isn't any such thing in your area, why not start it yourself and try to create a space that provides a feeling of community for helping animals? Or perhaps you can volunteer at the nearest animal sanctuary. Sanctuaries are popping up all over the place now, and you could take a non-vegan friend along so they can see these animals typically used for food up close. Some of my friends have even started their own mini-sanctuaries, where they take in rescue animals of their own, which gives them an enormous sense of gratification and happiness. There are so many ways to help create your own vegan community and to help nonhuman animals.

Assertive Vegan Communication

> "
>
> I just had a very difficult discussion with someone who came up with every excuse in the book for killing and eating animals. Some people are just too uncomfortable with the idea of change that they won't even listen to facts that we lay out for them. So I refused to let his childish comments with no logic upset me, and I maintained my good intentions to speak calmly but clearly about veganism. I have learned so much about veganism recently that I felt like I could deal with all of his rationalizations in a non-confrontational way, and for once, the conversation didn't turn into an argument, and I feel like he was actually listening in the end. I have found that the more calm and genuine I am, the better I'm able to reach others.
>
> "

As a psychologist, if there were one skill I could bestow upon every vegan in the universe, it would be *assertive communication*. Why is this so important? Well, because it's absolutely the most effective way to get your point across so that the other person actually listens and responds. To be assertive means to communicate your thoughts in an honest and straightforward way without holding in your feelings (passivity) or attacking the other person or raising your voice (aggression). To be assertive is to be respectful of yourself (by not holding things in), as well as respectful of the other person (by not attacking them).

To be assertive means to find that middle ground between passivity and aggression where you can express how you feel in a way that will be best received by others. Most young vegans I know probably fall closer to the passive end of the advocacy spectrum. To be passive means to avoid conflict. Oftentimes anger and other feelings are turned inward, and thoughts and feelings are not expressed. This is a big problem because when one is passive and "stuffs" their feelings, these feelings can build up inside, leading to emotional problems and physical health symptoms (e.g., upset stomach, headaches, muscle tension) and a greater likelihood for more aggressive outbursts later on. This is also problematic because when one is not assertive, their needs are often not met and no resolution to the issue can be achieved because their point of view was not expressed.

This is why it's so critical for young vegans to be assertive with others when talking about your feelings and beliefs. If you keep things all bottled up inside, it will only make you feel angry and depressed and increasingly prone to bouts of explosions. It's so important to let others know what's going on with you, even if they may not necessarily like or agree with what you have to say.

Applied to animal advocacy, the passive advocate may prefer to keep to themselves about their veganism. Perhaps they're afraid to talk about the ethics of using animals because they fear being ostracized or bullied for it. I know many vegans who are afraid of being thought of as an "angry vegan," so they don't talk about their veganism. This stereotype is promoted by non-vegans who would like vegans to remain silent about the abuse of animals. We as vegans should not let ourselves be silenced.

To be aggressive means to communicate in ways that are dominating or controlling of others. Aggressive communication can include blaming, name-calling, using put-downs, threatening others, getting loud, as well as non-verbal behaviors such as "staring down" someone or hovering over them in a threatening way. The problem with aggressive communication is that it puts the other person on the defensive, so they want to fight back. It may also frighten others, so they don't want to deal with you or listen to you. Of course, there are many other negative consequences of aggressive communication such as a loss of trust and closeness, loss of relationships, and people refusing to interact with you.

Aggressive communication in animal advocacy is obviously not an effective way to get your point across. When we express ourselves aggressively in our advocacy, others will be less inclined to listen to what we have to say, and they will assume that we're not being rational in our arguments. With aggressive communication, we may win an argument but lose opportunities to help others go vegan, so this approach is counterproductive.

Assertiveness skills are taught to clients in virtually every therapy approach for communication issues and family problems. Mastering these skills is also fundamental in managing one's anger and other emotions more effectively. They are also taught to those in various occupations because they're critical for building more positive relationships with customers, clients, and coworkers.

With assertive communication, we listen to the other person's perspective before offering our own point of view in a clear yet non-aggressive way. Setting limits is an important aspect of assertiveness. When we're assertive, we make it clear to others what our limits and boundaries are. To be assertive means that we avoid allowing others to mistreat us, just as we don't mistreat others.

How is this relevant for vegan advocacy? Our ability to persuade others to consider veganism is strongly influenced by our ability to connect with whomever we're communicating with. If we're passive and avoid directly discussing an issue, or if we're aggressive and attack the other person, there can't be a productive exchange of views and we won't develop the bond necessary to be truly influential. As I've discussed elsewhere,[1] if we want to help someone change their behavior, the relationship we form with them is perhaps the most important factor in our success or failure. In fact, a lot of scientific data in the social sciences indicates just that too; the relationship between the agent of change and the target of change has been shown to be more important than what is actually said.[2]

Being assertive does not mean giving in to others or being super polite all of the time. It involves expressing one's views and feelings in a way that is not abusive but still gets one's needs met. What we often find in family therapy is that openly discussing issues leads to a greater understanding and more positive relationships.

It's important to recognize that being more assertive is not something that comes naturally to everyone. Many of us have been raised to be more passive and to keep our feelings inside. Some may also feel vulnerable being more assertive because they may be more open to criticism and attacks if they speak out for themselves and for animals. Assertiveness is a skill that takes practice, and it may be helpful to be more assertive in manageable steps. I understand that being assertive is not always easy, and not all forms of animal advocacy may feel comfortable to you, but I still encourage you to try to push yourself to be more assertive. It may help you to find your voice as an animal advocate.

We can't force others to change if they're not open to our message. So try not to be discouraged when you use good assertiveness skills and the person you're communicating with doesn't respond in a positive manner. There's nothing we can do when others shut us out and refuse to engage with us.

One suggestion for increasing the likelihood of others listening to our assertive vegan message is to focus on our choices and ourselves. Rather than pointing out what others should be doing, we can simply tell them why we have chosen to go vegan and why it's important to us. Using "I statements" is an important strategy used in family therapy, where we focus on ourselves and how we feel, which will make us much less likely to be attacked by others because they will feel less criticized.

Psychological Abuse and Bullying

> " I really could use some advice. I'm getting so tired of getting so much abuse from other people when I speak up about veganism. I hate to say it, but some part of me wants to just be quiet about it—even though I know that doesn't help animals—just so the harassment will stop. I want to make people aware of the suffering of the animals regardless of the fact that I will be persecuted continuously for doing so. I feel like I'm at a crossroads and I don't really know what to do. "

> " Some people at school have made bullying me into a game. They are watching every bite I eat and then start rumors that I'm eating animals just to mess with me. They are harassing me on Facebook by posting images of dead animals and animal abuse under all of my posts. Yesterday a guy came and sat next to me at lunch, put his arm around me, and forced me to watch a video of a cow being slaughtered. It's giving me nightmares and I feel like I have to watch my back at all times. My friends say to stand up for myself, but I worry that will only make things worse. "

I regularly receive messages such as these from vegans who describe experiencing bullying behavior and psychological abuse from friends, family members, classmates, acquaintances, and strangers online. This is such an important issue for young vegans because this kind of behavior is almost unavoidable for many and it has a huge impact on their well-being.

A mountain of research has shown that psychologically abusive behaviors may have at least as large of a damaging effect on emotional and even physical well-being as physical abuse. This should not be surprising since the goal of psychological abuse and bullying is to affect the other person psychologically. Unfortunately, such abusive behavior often escalates over time and can lead to greater risk for physical violence as well. Psychological abuse is the most subtle and difficult to detect form of abuse, and therefore it is especially important to educate others about psychological abuse, because those who are experiencing it are often completely unaware.

Psychological abuse may come in different forms that can be distinguished based on the function that the behavior serves. For example, *denigration* behaviors include direct put-downs or other attempts used to lower the other person's sense of self-worth. Another form of psychological abuse involves *coercive* and *controlling* behaviors. These are behaviors intended to dictate what the other person does, using manipulation and bullying, to limit the other person's basic rights and freedoms, which lead to dependence and social isolation. An even more subtle form of psychological abuse—but at least equally damaging—involves *hostile withdrawal* behaviors, intended to punish the other person or leave them feeling insecure in the relationship. Then there are *dominance* and *intimidation* behaviors that are intended to invoke fear and force compliance.

Unfortunately, psychological abuse is all too common among people in general, with approximately half of those in the United States reporting the experience of this form of abuse.[1] A young vegan may be more likely than others to experience abusive behavior. As I discussed previously, others who aren't vegan don't like to be reminded that their behavior contributes to the harm of animals, and shame reactions may be angry and abusive. This abuse could take the form of online or in-person bullying, or more subtle attempts by loved ones to make the vegan feel like they're somehow harming the family or doing harm to themselves by being vegan.

Many animal advocates often have histories of experiencing trauma and abuse. For many of us, these traumatic experiences make us particularly sensitive to the injustices that nonhuman animals experience. It is damaging enough to be constantly exposed to the horrors of our collective animal use and the indifference to this injustice that so many hold. When we experience psychological abuse and have to deal with its repercussions, it can make it harder for us to take care of ourselves and to advocate for nonhuman animals.

So how do we cope with bullying and abusive behavior once we are able to recognize and label that abuse?

First, tell others about it. Talk to family members, school administrators, and your friends. Don't suffer in silence, and get the help that you need to directly deal with the situation to end the abuse. It's also very helpful to speak to others about it for your own mental health. Counseling can be very helpful, especially if you don't have others whom you feel you can talk to. For some, family counseling can also be helpful if the problems involve other family members. If you're feeling hopeless, helpless, or are thinking of suicide, don't hesitate to contact the National Suicide Prevention Lifeline at 1-800-273-TALK (8255).

Second, set clear limits with others. Let them know that you won't be bullied or abused by them. Block them on social media and otherwise remove them from your life so that you no longer need to be exposed to them. If it's somebody you live with or have a close personal relationship with, you will need to find a way to communicate your feelings and explain how the abuse is impacting you.

Third, when you recognize what they are trying to do with their abuse, you are armed to better deal with it. Psychological abuse and bullying are attempts to affect you psychologically, so when you see it happen, tell yourself that you won't let it get to you. What you tell yourself at these times is so critically important. Tell yourself that they can't impact how you feel about yourself and that their behavior will not stop you from confidently and assertively advocating for animals. Your strength and your confidence in yourself and your beliefs has nothing to do with them, and their abusiveness is their problem, not yours.

Finally, don't match abusive behavior and bullying with abuse of your own. Abuse is never justified and if you engage in this behavior it will likely only serve to escalate the situation and make things worse. There is nothing to be gained from lowering yourself to the level of abusive individuals. Be the bigger person and don't feed into an abusive pattern.

5

Tips for Communicating with Others about Veganism

> "
> So today my veganism pissed my best friend off so much that we are no longer speaking to each other. I have been careful not to bring up the subject of veganism around him at all because he has some relatives who are dairy farmers, but somehow he still tells me that I'm forcing my beliefs on him. So I was honest with him and told him that it's hypocritical to refuse to look at images or videos of what happens in animal agriculture while still funding the industries by eating meat and dairy. He's one of those people who claim to love animals but still eats them and won't listen to anything to the contrary.
> "

Beyond the issue of psychological abuse and bullying, young vegans are likely to encounter a lot of resistance to their veganism. Even if your loved ones are accepting of your veganism, you have almost certainly had unpleasant interactions with non-vegans. The easiest solution to this problem would be for the entire world to turn vegan, but until that happens here are seven tips to help you navigate these difficult waters.

1. Educate Yourself about Veganism
It's much easier to have discussions with challenging non-vegans if you have facts at your fingertips as well as responses to common questions and comments. Read as much as you can about

veganism—about the ethics, the scientific studies, environmental consequences, health benefits, and so forth—because, I assure you, there will be a time for you to discuss all of these things. There are also some helpful cheat sheets for common responses to challenges to veganism, including one titled "Eating Animals: Addressing Our Most Common Justifications," which can be found on the Free From Harm website.[1]

For new vegans, be prepared for it to take some time until you really feel like you can respond to all of the common questions, concerns, and arguments that you will encounter. Many of these, discussed in chapter 1, are absurd on the face of them and can be dismissed easily. Others may be more challenging if you're not familiar with the scientific literature or don't have a prepared response.

When in doubt during a discussion debating the merits of veganism, I encourage you to always bring it back to the ethical argument discussed previously: since we have no biological need to consume other animals and their secretions, and have no need to use nonhuman animals for any purpose, therefore it can't be ethical to do so. When a non-vegan attempts to bring the discussion in different directions, your best strategy is to always bring it back to this fundamental issue. No matter what cavepeople ate, no matter the size of our "canines," no matter the actual facts about human evolution, we have no need to be using animals in this day and age.

❝

Jim: This vegan stuff is all just stupid mumbo jumbo. Meat is food for humans and has been since the beginning of time. We're designed to eat meat; that's why we have these canines. You wouldn't go to the jungle and lecture to a cheetah not to eat those antelopes anymore, would you?

Sarah: Unlike cheetahs, humans have no biological need to eat other animals. It's not even healthy for us. Since it's unnecessary, it's not ethical. What humans ate a long time ago has no bearing on our current food choices. What matters is whether it's defensible to eat animals right now, in the current time, given the immense suffering it causes to animals and the destruction it does to the planet. There is no question that we have no need to kill and eat animals or their secretions, so it can't be ethical to continue to do so.

❞

2. RECOGNIZE YOUR TRIGGERS

For many of us, there may be one question or comment that is especially irksome; for example, "What about the lives of the plants that you kill?" It's a good idea to really think about the kinds of situations and comments that can set you off and get you upset. If you're aware of your triggers, you can be prepared when the situation arises. Understand that when this happens, it might be a good idea to take a break from the conversation or do something to cool down rather than lose your composure.

In the area of anger management, this is referred to as a "time out." The better able we are to recognize as early as possible that we're starting to get angry, the better able we will be to short-circuit the anger response and deal with the situation in a productive way. In addition to paying attention to the kinds of situations that may be especially upsetting to you, it's also very helpful for you to try to become aware of the early warning signs that you're starting to get upset or angry.

Anger warning signs can be physiological or can involve certain feelings and thoughts. Physiological signs of anger might include increased heart rate, teeth clenching, muscles tightening, blood rushing, rapid breathing, sweating, headache, stomach pain, trembling, and so forth.

Common feelings that underlie anger are disgust, rage, hurt, sadness, embarrassment, frustration, humiliation, and the like. It's helpful to be aware of the feelings other than anger, because when we get angry with others, there are almost always other feelings underneath that anger that we need to be aware of and that we may want to communicate to the other person.

It's very helpful to be aware of our thoughts when we're starting to get angry, because our thoughts are what often fuel our anger. For many of us, when we're starting to get angry, our thoughts begin to race, and they usually race in a negative direction. For example, we begin to think that the other person is just trying to upset us, that they are not on our side, or that they're purposely trying to harm us in some way. If we can recognize and catch these negative thoughts early on and replace them with more positive thoughts, we will deal with the situation better.

When a non-vegan says something upsetting to you, what you tell yourself makes all the difference for how you'll respond. Instead of telling yourself that this person is an ignorant jerk, remind yourself that you once held similar beliefs as that person before you were vegan, or tell yourself that you're simply not going to let this person ruin your day. Or you could take a totally Zen approach and thank the person for providing you with a growth experience.

3. Show that You're Listening

Most people don't realize that the most important communication skill is the ability to listen. This can be a challenge when you vehemently disagree with the other person, but if they see that you're listening to them, they will be more receptive to hearing out your point of view.

So how do we help others feel heard? First and foremost, we need to have a listening mindset where understanding the other person takes priority. Try to first hear the other person out without offering your views. Once they feel that you understand what they are saying, it will be much easier for you to communicate your own opinions.

There are some other simple strategies you can use that can go a long way toward better two-way communication. First, you can try to paraphrase what people are saying to you. To paraphrase means to repeat back what they have said to you, using your own words to convey that you understood the meaning behind what they said.

Example phrases to start paraphrasing are:

"What I hear you saying is ..."
"So you feel ..."
"So what you want is ..."

I know this might be a bit uncomfortable to say if you're not used to paraphrasing, but once you get in the habit, it gets a lot easier and you may find that people respond really positively to it. When I was first studying to be a clinical psychologist, I learned to use paraphrasing to help my patients feel understood, and it felt very awkward at first. But then I soon realized that my patients loved it when I paraphrased; they really saw that I was listening to them, which made them more likely to follow my advice.

Another strategy to show someone that you're listening is to ask, without judging or accusing, what the other person is feeling. When you have a question in mind, ask yourself whether the question is designed to prove your point or whether it is an honest attempt to understand the other person. Try not to frame questions as a disguised attempt to prove a point.

The highest level of listening is when you can show that you understand where the other person is coming from, even if you don't agree with them. When you can demonstrate that you understand why the other person might think and feel the way they do, the other person may be less combative and more likely to have a productive conversation. Just because you're validating the other person does not mean that you agree with them. For example, you can demonstrate understanding that a certain person was socialized to consume animals, while still disagreeing about the ethics of funding the needless killing of nonhuman animals.

So next time you want to interrupt a non-vegan's comment and hastily offer your response, try to reflect back what they're saying first to show you heard them, and try to find something that you can validate about what they're saying, so long that you don't hurt your vegan message. Then you can present your vegan point and the other person may actually listen to what you have to say.

4. Learn When to End the Discussion

Sometimes people aren't really looking to have a legitimate exchange of ideas, but, rather, are looking for a "gotcha" moment where your whole vegan world will come tumbling down (something that never actually happens, but it doesn't stop them from trying). When someone is clearly not looking for a real discussion, it's perfectly fine to let them know that you're not going to engage with them.

Pretty much any vegan will tell you that they have wasted a lot of time trying to convince others of the merits of veganism when the other person clearly had no interest in really learning about veganism. My advice is to try to ascertain, early on in the discussion, whether the other person is really interested in an exchange of ideas about the issue, or if they just want to try to tell you that you're wrong for being vegan. If it's the latter and not the former, there is nothing that can really be gained by continuing to engage.

In clinical psychology, there is a model of behavioral change called the "Stages of Change Model" that is very influential when we're trying to help others change problem behaviors. A central tenet of the model is that we can be most effective as advocates if we can recognize where the other person is in terms of their readiness for changing and for hearing other points of view. If someone is in the "precontemplation" stage, it means that they're not even considering or thinking about changing a behavior and that they are unlikely to make the change anytime soon. Those who are in this earliest stage of change will be most likely to talk about some of the common justifications for animal use I mentioned previously, such as human evolution, what cave-people ate, human canine teeth, and so forth.

I'm not necessarily saying that you should never engage with someone who is not considering going vegan at the present time, but rather try to determine if the conversation is productive or if it's just upsetting you. If nothing is being gained by the conversation, it's always best to let the other person know that you don't feel like the conversation is productive and you can revisit the discussion at some later time if they seriously want to talk about it.

5. GET INVOLVED WITH ACTIVISM AND OTHERS WHO SHARE YOUR VEGAN PERSPECTIVE

I have personally found that I'm much better able to deal with challenging non-vegans when I feel that I'm doing good work focused on preventing harm to nonhuman animals. When I'm engaging in various forms of vegan education and advocacy, I can take comfort in the fact that I'm doing what I can for the cause, and I feel like I'm doing something meaningful with real-life consequences.

This is actually a lesson that I learned during my graduate school training. I used to be prone to depression, which got worse when I was in graduate school dealing with a lot of stressful situations, and felt like I was at a breaking point. As luck would have it, I was doing a practicum at the time, working with psychiatric inpatients at a hospital. I was conducting therapy with folks with severe long-standing problems, such as schizophrenia and other psychotic disorders, and they were too impaired to be able to function on the outside. I really worked hard to try to connect with and understand my patients, to learn their language so to speak, and I believe I did a very good job at that and made progress with some patients when it hadn't been thought possible. Eventually, I'd notice that when I walked into the ward several patients would light up and were so happy to see me, and they'd come up to talk to me. Then I began to notice that I wasn't feeling so depressed anymore, and I realized that my patients were helping me more than I could ever have helped them. Doing something meaningful and helping other people can truly be the best therapy.

For this reason, if you feel like you're making a difference in the lives of nonhuman animals and are helping to make the world a better place overall, you will likely feel happier and less frustrated when dealing with day-to-day challenges. Getting involved with animal activism—in whatever way you feel comfortable with and that makes best use of your specific interests and talents—will have the double benefit of helping the larger cause and also helping you because your life will have more meaning.

I also think that it's important for all vegans to seek out other vegans and to build their own personal community, whether it's in person or online. Go to vegan meet-ups, get involved with online vegan groups, go to veg fests—whatever makes you feel most connected to likeminded individuals. While we can't live in an entirely vegan world just yet, we do have control over whom we spend our time with, and there will undoubtedly be times when you feel exasperated and fed up with those who are not yet aware of the harm done to animals, and you may want to vent or otherwise communicate with others who best understand veganism.

6. We Can't Force Change (Unfortunately)

As much as we want to promote veganism and prevent needless violence toward other animals and our planet, if you try to force the issue too strongly, it might end up having the reverse effect. At some point, you will have done all that you can do to raise awareness (though you may have planted a seed that takes root in their mind for later growth).

Going back to the Stages of Change model, we will be unlikely to change those who are completely resistant to the idea of change. This can be extremely frustrating, especially when we're trying to convince our loved ones of the importance of going vegan and minimizing the harm that we do to nonhuman animals. But there comes a point where our continued efforts only serve to make it less likely for the other person to listen to our perspective, and we can do harm to relationships, which will also make us less able to have an influence.

This is a basic rule of psychology that I have learned. I have come to the understanding that I can't necessarily change my patients if they're unwilling to change themselves. I try to encourage them to take the next steps toward nonviolent goals, but if they're unwilling to join with me in developing that long-term goal, there is only so much I can do.

It's important that we as advocates don't put too much pressure on ourselves to change others, because this is very difficult to do and some people will not change no matter what we say or do. Bringing about change can be a long and subtle process, but we should always bear in mind that we may be helping to plant seeds and help others move closer to veganism even if it's not readily observable or apparent.

7. Give Others the Benefit of the Doubt

Too often I see young vegans with overly low expectations of others. For example, I often see them express how they don't confide in their families about what's going on with them, be it depression or anxiety or something else, because they don't want to burden them or don't think they will understand. While those around us might disappoint us at times, it's better to assume the best from them than the worst. When we truly need others, they may come through for us and surprise us by really listening and trying to help.

The same applies to our advocacy. If we assume that others won't be receptive to our message, then we will seek and find the worst in their response and we will be less effective in our advocacy. So try to avoid developing an overly cynical mindset when communicating with others, because that is not conducive to effective communication or advocacy.

6

Challenges Communicating with Loved Ones

> **"**
>
> I'm in tears as I write this because it's impossible for me to have a good relationship with my mother right now. This morning she was telling me how proud she was from telling a hunter that he would end up being a deer in his next life. I told her that at least those animals he killed experienced some kind of freedom before being needlessly killed, while she buys from a grocery store dead animals who have been enslaved, raped, and imprisoned their entire short lives. It escalated and we ended up yelling at each other for like an hour. I don't know what to do. I feel like I hate my mother right now.
>
> **"**

As we all know, communication can intensify quicker when it involves family members or others whom we are close to. This can make discussions related to veganism much more upsetting and have a greater likelihood of conflict. I have seen some cases of families who are completely accepting of their family member's veganism, in rare cases with the whole family going vegan. I will admit that I'm jealous of those families because it is certainly not the norm, and is not the case in my family.

What can make communication with non-vegan loved ones particularly challenging is that we often have high expectations for them. We may know them as kind people who have always cared about others and issues of justice. So how, then, can we reconcile the fact that they continue to fund abusive animal industries even when we provide them with all of the information anyone could possibly need to make more ethical choices? This is the question that is at the heart of the matter for a lot of family conflicts among vegans, particularly when they first make the transition.

Sometimes we can also feel rejected by our non-vegan loved ones because we think that if they really understand our veganism, they'd go vegan too since there is no justification for the needless killing of animals. The vegan advocate wants so much for their loved ones to understand their advocacy for animals, because it is a huge part of who they are as a person. Perhaps they're accustomed to being able to share with their loved ones their feelings about various issues and their beliefs overall, and now find that they have difficulty connecting in this way because their loved ones may reject their veganism.

As mentioned earlier, it may be particularly helpful to think of others, including our loved ones, as "pre-vegans," meaning that we have the expectation that they will eventually be vegan, but they haven't gotten there yet.[1] This perspective is more hopeful than thinking of our loved ones as somehow ignorant or bad, and it reminds us that we, too (in most cases), were non-vegan at one point. While we have learned to eliminate the false distinctions between different sentient beings, those all around us have not, and therefore they really do not truly understand our perspective. The only way for them to really know is for us to communicate that to them in a clear way. We need to let them know how we are changing and what we have learned. Some will resist listening to us, and there is nothing we can do about that. Others may have real interest and show a more supportive response.

Thinking of our loved ones as pre-vegans doesn't mean that we should avoid advocating for animals. On the contrary, we should let our families know how we feel about the harm we do to animals and why we're strong in our convictions, using all of the communication strategies discussed previously. Perhaps most importantly, we should let our loved ones know how we feel when it comes to our veganism and their response to our veganism. If we feel hurt or disappointed by their reaction, we should let them know that in an assertive, non-aggressive way. It's totally reasonable for us to be disappointed with our loved ones and their response to us, but how we convey that disappointment and other feelings we're experiencing will go a long way toward getting to a place of greater understanding.

In chapter 3, I discussed the importance of establishing boundaries for assertive communication with others, and this may be especially helpful with loved ones because it can help avoid major blowups. Having an understanding of what our limits are and cutting off conversations that may be especially upsetting or counterproductive are important aspects of being able to communicate effectively with people we care about.

For example, it may mean that we need to avoid certain events that we know will be especially upsetting for us and have a high likelihood of conflict, such as barbecues or even major holidays. While it may be difficult to miss such events, it may be what's truly necessary based on our own limits and feelings. The important thing is to show respect for our loved ones by letting them know how we feel in a clear and non-aggressive way, as well as respect ourselves by not holding in all of our feelings. Remember that there are no right or wrong feelings, and how one handles a difficult situation with loved ones may work better for them, while a completely different approach might work better for someone else.

While setting boundaries and having awareness of our limits is important, at the same time, we should be careful not to avoid our loved ones altogether if we want to remain close with them. For us to feel close to others, there needs to be open communication and the sharing of feelings. So be careful not to shut others out completely if you want to maintain a close relationship.

As discussed in chapter 5, the more that we know about issues related to veganism, the more confident we will be across a range of interactions, and over time, we may find that our discussions become less heated because we have greater confidence in what we're saying. I myself, as a clinical psychologist and communication skills expert, had difficulties communicating with family members when I first went vegan. There were times when my loved ones brought up justifications for using animals that I wasn't expecting and didn't have a ready response for, which was frustrating to me, and I didn't always respond in a helpful way. After some time, no issue or argument for using animals came as a surprise, and it was easy to respond to anything that might be thrown my way.

For any close relationship, we work to accept what we can about the other person, while also working to change what we can change. Acceptance and change are the cornerstones for some of the most effective therapy approaches for families.[2] To have continued positive relationships with non-vegan loved ones, the animal advocate might need to continually work to accept that the other person may not change, at least in the short term. I know many highly influential vegans who have confided that communicating with loved ones about animal use was an ongoing long, difficult process. While we should never accept the exploitation of animals as morally defensible, it is entirely up to us as to whether we continue to accept the non-vegan loved ones into our lives and work toward greater mutual understanding and closeness.

7

Vegan Dating

> **"**
>
> I need some help coping with my non-vegan partner. He tells me that it's great that I care so much about animals, but he told me not to try to force my beliefs on him. He told me today that he's never going vegan so I shouldn't get my hopes up. I started balling right there. Does anyone have any tips on how to deal with anger toward our partners when they are being narrow-minded and ignorant as hell?
>
> **"**

This is admittedly the toughest chapter for me to write because I was very lucky in the vegan dating department. When I met my wife, I was on a plant-based diet and she was not. In fact, on our very first date, much to my dismay, she ordered and ate a dead fish at the fancy restaurant that I took her to, and that was the last time she ever ate animal flesh. Not too long after that, we both went truly vegan together. I conveyed to her how important it was to me for us to be vegan, and she truly listened and looked into it, and decided it was the right thing to do.

If my wife hadn't have been so open to veganism, I'm sure we wouldn't be married right now. When we think of our use of animals as an issue of social justice, it's hard to fathom the idea of spending one's time (or one's life) with someone who regularly and knowingly contributes to that injustice. It is one thing when the non-vegan is simply not aware of all the issues involved. When we have spent time with them, however, and they have all of the information and still remain non-vegan, that's a big problem and a serious warning sign about relationship compatibility.

So my first tip for dating for vegans would be to find another vegan to date! That would certainly be easiest. My wife and I own Vegan Publishers and we are a team when it comes to vegan advocacy and getting out the vegan message. We're better vegan advocates together than separately, and we both share the philosophy that we should try to do the most good that we can and the least harm while we're on this planet.

That said, this might be easier said than done, especially when vegans are not necessarily in abundance when we get outside of major urban areas. I often hear and read stories from vegans who really struggle with their non-vegan partners around issues of animal use and abuse. This is becoming less and less of an issue as our numbers are growing, and there are more and more ways to meet vegan partners online, but nonetheless I regularly hear how hard it is to meet other vegan singles, regardless of gender or sexual orientation. Some vegans will date someone who has certain qualities that suggest they may be inclined to going vegan down the road even if they are not vegan yet, such as being compassionate, open-minded, or socially and politically progressive.

If you do choose to date a non-vegan, it's helpful to keep in mind all of the communication tips discussed in this book. Perhaps most importantly, keep the lines of communication open. Let the other person know how you feel about things, including their use of animals, and don't feel like you need to tiptoe around them. You are vegan and should be proud of that; you should never feel like you need to silence yourself to keep others happy.

Does that mean that you should greet your partner every morning with a clip from *Earthlings* (a documentary known as the "vegan maker")? Probably not, because just repeating something again and again is not necessarily an effective strategy to compel others to change. You may have to pick and choose your spots for talking about veganism, and recognize good timing for when to express your feelings to your partner.

Sometimes, expectations that couples share with each other can make a big difference. For example, if both members of a married couple were non-vegan before their marriage and then one partner goes vegan, this can be especially difficult because there was no expectation before the marriage that either would go vegan.

For other couples, one partner may decide that they would not marry their non-vegan partner until they make the vegan transition. In this case, the expectations are made clear up front before a larger commitment is made.

One might say, "What my partner eats is none of my business." The problem with that, though, is that animals are not objects. They are sentient beings who want to live just as much as we do. So if one chooses to participate in funding an industry that inflicts injustice upon others, it is not simply a food choice but rather a direct participation in the oppression of others. We are certainly justified to tell our partners that we would have difficulty being with someone who knowingly harms nonhuman animals, just like we would be justified to let them know that we would have difficulty with someone knowingly harming other humans.

I have seen some couples get creative when it comes to navigating household duties, where the non-vegan partner does their own shopping and their own cooking. Many couples appear to pull off this sort of arrangement and they say that it works for them. For any relationship, the key is open communication and having an understanding that works for them.

Things get even more complicated when children are involved if one of the members of the couple is non-vegan. I believe that raising a child vegan from birth is a great gift that we can give them. When we do this, we opt out of socializing them into a paradigm that does direct harm to others. The child can start off on the right foot where they view nonhuman animals as worthy of ethical consideration, and they will learn a philosophy of nonviolence from the very start. Almost all of us vegans have had to unlearn what we were taught about nonhuman animals in order to make the vegan transition.

This is relevant because sometimes couples have disagreements about whether their child should be raised vegan. If we believe that minimizing the harm we do to animals is a moral imperative, then raising our child as non-vegan should be a non-starter. This can, of course, create a great deal of stress in the relationship and can be a test of our communication and emotional expression abilities.

In the end, all successful relationships involve some degree of acceptance of the other person and self-change. It is up for us to decide what we can accept in our partners, and what we are willing to work on changing. In a perfect world, we will all strive to change in the direction of veganism and nonviolence.

Masculinity, Sex, and Veganism

A report published in the *Journal of Consumer Research* showed that in a number of experiments, research participants (most from the United States and Great Britain) rated animal flesh as more "masculine" than other foods, and vegetables were rated as more "feminine."[1] The top five most masculine foods were (1) medium-rare steak, (2) hamburger, (3) well-done steak, (4) beef chili, and (5) chicken. Participants also rated those who do not eat animals as less masculine and more feminine than animal consumers.

This study highlights the notion of vegan men being somehow more feminine than non-vegan men. Across a number of cultures, eating animal flesh is associated with being a masculine trait in men, and abstaining from flesh eating is associated with femininity in men. Most vegan men have been teased by male friends or family members with comments such as, "Real men don't eat tofu," or "Be a man—have some meat."

A common reaction among vegan men to such teasing is one of disbelief, since to them the killing and eating of defenseless cows and pigs does not represent strength and virility. Moreover, these toxic notions of masculinity are damaging on many levels and are responsible for a lot of needless violence toward women, people in the LGBTQIA community, and other vulnerable individuals. The notion that being more masculine is something that all men should strive for, and that masculinity is viewed as a positive trait while femininity is a negative one, is not only sexist and transphobic, but it also perpetuates a sort of toxic masculinity that underlies many problems in our society.

Related to the claim that veganism is somehow feminizing is the controversy around soy consumption in men. Soy contains isoflavones, which are selective estrogen receptor modulators. Contrary to popular belief, isoflavones are not the same thing as the female sex hormone estrogen, since it binds differently to estrogen receptors in cells.[2] Research also shows that human consumption of soy and isoflavones does not increase estrogen levels,[3] reduce testosterone levels,[4] or lower sperm count,[5] again contrary to popular beliefs about the impacts of soy on men's reproductive health and masculinity. Soy has been the target of a marketing campaign by organizations sympathetic to the meat and dairy industries, so we really need to consider the scientific evidence when evaluating the truth about this bean.

If you have any doubt about whether vegans can be healthy and strong, just take a look at all of the plant-based athletes who have had amazing success, such as tennis player Serena Williams, ultramarathon runner Scott Jurek, Mr. Universe Barny du Plessis, or world record holding vegan strongman Patrik Baboumian. There are some great social media pages for vegan athletes as well, such as "Vegan Bodybuilding & Fitness." If this is of interest to you, there is an enormous vegan fitness community who would welcome you in and teach you all that you could ever want to learn about how to be a fit and healthy vegan athlete or to just stay in shape.

There is good reason to believe that veganism may promote enhanced sexual functioning. Physiologically, healthy arteries are key for providing pressurized blood to the penis and clitoris, and a vegan diet is known to be good for healthy blood vessels. The lower cholesterol levels in a vegan diet and presence of the amino acid L-arginine promote healthy blood flow, and in turn, better sexual functioning.[6] Leafy greens like spinach and broccoli are also high in magnesium, folate, and nitrate, which contribute to healthy blood flow. Vegan diets rich in antioxidants also may have a positive effect on mood,[7] which may be linked to higher sex drive. Finally, fruits and vegetables high in water content, such as cucumber, cantaloupe, and watermelon, and foods high in Omega 3, such as sunflower seeds, may contribute to greater lubrication of the skin, which may have sexual benefits.

9

Tips for Animal Advocacy

> Today I presented my final project about the cruelty of the egg industry, and I talked about the moral imperative of veganism. Afterwards, four different people told me that it inspired them to look into veganism more, and one even said that he made the decision to go vegan right then and there! I presented to probably around fifty people, but am so happy that I can inspire people to make such an important change that will save so many lives. Now I know that people can change if we find a way to reach them through direct vegan education and compassion, and if they're ready to hear our message.

I've written another book that applies principles of clinical psychology to animal advocacy called *Motivational Methods for Vegan Advocacy: A Clinical Psychology Perspective*. A primary reason I wrote it was because there is so much young energy flowing into the animal advocacy movement and I want to help make sure that this great energy is going in the right direction. Some of the main points I made in that book are summarized throughout this book. Below I offer some central tips that I believe can be helpful for any animal advocate to consider. For a fuller discussion of these points, and for more tips on how to motivate apparently unmotivated non-vegans, I encourage you to check out *Motivational Methods*.

PROMOTE VEGANISM

This may seem to go without saying, but unfortunately some of the leaders in the animal movement are reluctant to unequivocally promote veganism, and instead ask others to merely "go veg" or "go vegetarian" or to only cut back on using animals. Despite what anyone might tell you, there is absolutely no evidence that these more watered down approaches are effective; there is actually a lot that we know about behavioral change to believe that this is the wrong way to go.

The obvious problem with that strategy is that if we want to have a vegan world, we need to promote veganism. If we want people to end violence, we need to promote nonviolence, not violence reduction. In the field of clinical psychology, developing clear long-term end goals have been shown time and time again to be absolutely crucial, and these goals are most effective when they are challenging. So just asking others to "do your best" is not a particularly effective strategy because we're not helping the other person develop a clear goal to work toward.

The ethical argument for veganism—that we have no need to use and kill animals and therefore it can't be ethical—is our strongest one. Any time we get away from this central message, we water it down and make it harder for others to see the moral imperative of veganism.

Some will argue that it's a journey for some people to go vegan and that a "baby steps" approach worked for them. I know it took me a while to go fully vegan, but I would never advocate for someone to take baby steps. If we openly talk to others about veganism, it may accelerate the process of them going vegan. I truly believe that if someone talked to me about veganism earlier, I would have gone vegan much sooner. When we engage in vegan education, others may still take baby steps in getting there, but they decide on those baby steps, not us. Again, there is no evidence whatsoever that promoting baby steps is any more effective than when we promote veganism.

The larger problem with telling others that they should simply "cut down on" animal use is that it promotes the view that it's acceptable to use animals in moderation. This is damaging for the larger vegan movement because it reinforces social norms about animal harm. We won't change the dominant paradigm—where people think it's okay to needlessly kill animals—if we are putting out views that support this paradigm.

What it comes down to is our use of animals is an issue of social justice, and this needless torture and killing is a gross injustice. We would never suggest to a domestic abuser that he simply cut down on his abuse, because that would be an injustice to the victims. The same logic applies to animal advocacy. If we want to promote justice for *all* animals, we must promote veganism and not be apologetic about it. We can do this in a motivational way, which I discuss next.

CONSIDER OTHERS' READINESS FOR CHANGE

Not everyone will be receptive to a vegan message, of course. In the field of clinical psychology, there is literature showing that people may be at various stages with respect to their readiness for changing any behavior. Our ability to help them change may depend on whether we're able to clearly recognize their level of readiness and match our approach to that level.

For example, if somebody is not currently considering going vegan and it's not even on their radar, consciousness-raising efforts to make them aware of the harm we do to nonhuman animals, and to counter common justifications for animal use, may be particularly effective. When the individual is considering veganism but is still unsure about making the transition, here we can discuss the barriers that may be getting in the way, and emphasize the reasons in favor of changing. When the other person has made the decision to go vegan and needs help in getting there, providing recipes and shopping tips might be most helpful. Of course, when the person has gone vegan, helping them find a network supportive of their veganism can be especially important.

Most of us have had the experience of trying to help someone go vegan and our efforts don't seem to work. No matter what we may say or do to try to convince the other to go vegan, they seem unmoved. Don't get discouraged when this happens. It doesn't mean that the person will never change, just that they're not ready to hear the vegan message at this time. It may do no good to continue trying to force the issue here; if they're "dug in" and are shutting you out, pushing harder will not necessarily bring about change. Sometimes it's best to simply plant seeds and move on and find someone who may be more interested in changing.

Try not to put too much pressure on yourself to help others go vegan. As a psychologist, I recognize that I won't have a breakthrough with my patients every session, just like I will not convince someone to go vegan during every interaction. We all want to help end the horrific animal abuse that is all around us, but at the same time, we need to recognize that we are not going to change others overnight. The more pressure we put on ourselves, the more likely that frustration and depression will set in, which will make it harder for us to be effective advocates.

Relationships Are Important

There is a wealth of research in the area of clinical psychology to show that the more we are able to develop a positive relationship with the person whom we're trying to help change, the more they will change. The same should hold true in animal advocacy. The better we're able to join with the non-vegan in working toward a vegan goal, the more likely it is that they will go vegan.

How do we best develop positive relationships with non-vegans? Like I discussed in chapter 5, showing others that we are listening to them, and showing that we can understand why they might feel how they do (even if we disagree), can open the door for more positive communication. There is a reason that the first thing they teach workers for various jobs, like sales, is how to show someone that they're listening to them and understanding their perspective. This is because when someone feels like their views are understood and valued, they will be more inclined to like the other person and listen to them.

Just liking someone isn't enough, however, to bring about change. Developing a positive relationship with a non-vegan isn't enough to make them change; it needs to also involve a vegan end goal. This is where some advocates seem to get it fundamentally wrong. They present weak vegan messages because they fear it will be off-putting to non-vegans who reject that message, which serves to undermine their advocacy in general.

It is entirely possible to put out clear vegan messages that promote an end to our animal use while at the same time showing respect for others and connecting with them, setting the stage for behavioral change. As someone who works with domestic violence perpetrators, this is something that I do on a daily basis, and my clients actually appreciate when I am honest with them and am also non-attacking about their need to change. The same general approach is what's best for animal advocacy.

BE MORALLY CONSISTENT

If we really want others to take us seriously when we make the case that the needless use of nonhuman animals is a social justice issue, we need to demonstrate that we care about other issues of social justice too. If we convey that we only care about nonhuman animals and not injustice experience by marginalized groups of humans, we are demonstrating moral inconsistency and are thus weakening our own vegan message.

Veganism does not give us a free pass when it comes to our own oppressive behaviors either. I have run across racist and sexist vegans, for example, who seem to think that as long as they are advocating for nonhuman animals, they can express views harmful to other humans. Our movement would be better off without these vegans who make us look like a joke and who make it even more difficult for us to reach those in other social justice movements who might otherwise be receptive to our message and join us in fighting injustice.

Once we go vegan, our learning and development as activists does not end. We should always strive to have more understanding of various forms of oppression and learn to advocate for justice clearly and in an informed manner. There is nothing to be gained from showing indifference to the suffering and oppression of others, and a lot to lose. If we ever hope to get beyond the margins in animal advocacy and create a vibrant and inclusive mainstream animal rights movement, we need to bring in other social justice advocates who resonate with our message.

Part of demonstrating regard for other marginalized groups is to be mindful of the language and analogies that we use. For example, it is common for white vegans to use black slavery analogies in an attempt to convey that nonhuman animals experience a form of slavery, as their bodies are used as property for human gain. The fundamental problem with using this kind of comparison is that it appropriates a group's history of oppression and insensitively evokes images that are extremely upsetting and offensive to a large population of people whose oppression is historically rooted in their "animalization." Moreover, human slavery still exists and the legacy of slavery is very much with us today.

An important aspect of being an effective advocate is to be mindful of how others are receiving us. There is nothing to be gained by giving the impression that we are insensitive, indifferent, or unknowledgeable when it comes to others' experiences of injustice and oppression. When we communicate using analogies and concepts that others can connect to, that lead to a lowering of others' defenses and an increase in their receptiveness to our message, we will be better able to help others make the changes that are needed to prevent harm to nonhuman animals.

Trauma in Animal Advocacy

> "
>
> Graphic videos of animal abuse are just too much for me. I became a vegan early on because eating flesh and the bodily fluids of animals were just never appealing to me and I always knew it was wrong to kill and eat them. I also recognize that every animal has an individual personality and a will to live, just like we do. Whenever I see the animals actually being tortured and killed for all of these "products" that we don't even need, I feel completely helpless. Then I feel angry with those who still eat animals and who buy fur, and I just want everyone to stop the madness. Then I begin to feel like everybody is cruel and heartless. I'm sure it helps some people become convinced that these cruel acts need to change, but for me, my heart just breaks over and over every time I see them, and I have a hard time not feeling angry and jaded.
>
> "

I am not aware of any research on this issue, but it is likely that animal advocates are at higher risk for experiencing trauma. After all, many of us became vegans and animal advocates in part because our own exposure to abuse and violence among humans sensitized us to abuse and violence toward nonhuman animals. We don't want to see the most defenseless among us be harmed unnecessarily.

Animal advocates are essentially exposed to trauma by definition. We can't advocate for animals without bearing witness to the trauma that they experience. Whether it's on our social media feeds, through exposure to our loved ones who may contribute to animal harm, or just a trip to the grocery store, violence and trauma are all around us. One of the side effects of being more aware about the harm society inflicts upon animals is that we're repeatedly exposed to trauma.

This trauma exposure can wear on us and negatively impact our overall sense of well-being. We care so much about the trauma inflicted on nonhuman animals, and the fact that we can only do so much to immediately end this trauma is devastating to many of us.

It goes without saying that trauma exposure places us at risk for a variety of mental health issues, such as depression and posttraumatic stress disorder. Some may turn to alcohol or other substances to try to avoid these trauma reminders and numb the pain. Some may also cope with these problems by turning their frustration and depression outward, resulting in difficulties with anger and aggression.

It is important for all of us to be aware of how we are doing emotionally and to decide for ourselves what degree of trauma exposure, if any, we are able to withstand. We as vegans must make sure that we're taking good care of ourselves and are aware of our limits when it comes to how much exposure to trauma is healthy for us to withstand. This might mean we need to limit exposure to certain social media pages, certain individuals, and perhaps even some conversations if we feel that it's beyond our capacity to cope with them well.

We are not able to best help nonhuman animals if we are incapacitated with sadness and grief as we are exposed to the trauma inflicted on them. Part of learning about how to be a good animal advocate is learning how best to take care of ourselves, both physically and emotionally, and surrounding ourselves with a supportive network that we can reach out to when we feel sad, frustrated, or a range of other negative emotions.

Self-care is not something that young people are usually taught, but it's something that will help you for the rest of your life, so there's no better time than now to think about how you can best make sure that you're doing what you need to do to be happy and healthy. This might mean finding ways to reduce stress by exercising more often, talking to friends more for support, doing fun things that you enjoy, finding ways to blow off steam, or something else. It might mean being careful about whom you surround yourself with and limiting exposure to harmful people. It might mean getting treatment that you need for emotional or physical health issues. It's really different for everyone, but the key is to figure out what you need to do to take good care of yourself.

Trauma can also impact how we view others, particularly non-vegans. For some vegans, upon developing awareness about what our society does to animals, and with the knowledge that others all around them directly contribute to this harm, they develop an extremely negative view of people in general. I often hear animal advocates say things like "people are just horrible," and "the world would be better off if humans were just wiped off the face of the earth."

While it's of course true that humans are a destructive species, when we develop a cynical view of others, we will be more likely to miss out on opportunities for providing vegan education and helping them go vegan. We will be most impactful as advocates if we can retain a hopeful view of others and find ways to reach them. If we assume the worst about non-vegans, we may not have the best mindset to help them change.

In other words, we can't help others go vegan if we're constantly skeptical of them and think of them as terrible people. We can't help others go vegan if we jump down their throats immediately when they present us with seemingly absurd justifications for animal use. Our best hope of creating a vegan world is to calmly but passionately present our case in a rational and compassionate way, presenting ourselves as people who simply want to prevent needless violence, trauma, and killing of animals.

I encourage you to find help if you feel stuck in a state of negativity and hopelessness. If you find yourself struggling with these issues it is important to consider seeking a counselor or someone who can help you work through your trauma and associated thoughts and feelings. You can also seek various forms of family therapy or other kinds of supportive interventions if you believe that's a better fit. If you do reach out for help, it might also be a good idea to do some research beforehand and make sure that the counselor is vegan-friendly, if not vegan themselves. Given societal views on veganism, this might not be easy, but it is worth doing this kind of checking beforehand to avoid disappointments and negative interactions in counseling.

Again, if you are feeling suicidal, it's critical that you tell someone about it. Feelings of depression are particularly likely to happen when one first goes vegan while learning about all of the cruelty that we inflict upon nonhuman animals. Keep in mind that a lot of people have felt exactly the same way that you do, and they're so very happy that they didn't harm or kill themselves, and they live happy lives today. I've spoken with so many patients who were suicidal at one point and now realize that they would have missed out on an entire lifetime if they had gone through with it.

CASE EXAMPLE

Jemma is a twenty-two-year-old bisexual, black, vegan woman. As a child, she was regularly ridiculed by her father, who called her a "dyke" and a "freak" on a daily basis. Her uncle sexually assaulted her when she was twelve, and none of her family believed or supported her when she spoke out. She was also teased at school for being "different" than the other kids, and she often had suicidal thoughts growing up. At the age of sixteen she moved in with her grandmother, and she moved out and got her own place when she was eighteen. Soon after that, she read *The Sexual Politics of Meat: A Feminist Vegetarian Critical Theory*[1] and went vegan. She has since been in several failed relationships and mostly keeps to herself because she has a difficult time being around others and doesn't feel like she can trust anyone given all of the abuse she's experienced in her life. She also keeps her veganism mostly to herself because she's triggered when others tease her for being vegan or when she comes across images of harmed animals.

Jemma seems to be suffering from symptoms of depression and posttraumatic stress disorder, and it would be a good idea for her to seek an evaluation with a professional who might be able to help her with these problems. Her perceptions of others are understandably skeptical and negative, and she may need assistance getting to a place where she can learn not to assume the worst in others. This will likely be a difficult but potentially life-changing process. Seeking support in the pro-intersectional vegan community may also help Jemma, as social interaction can buffer the effects of stress and trauma on one's well-being. Perhaps if she learns that there are some people out there whom she can learn to trust, she will develop a more hopeful and positive perspective. She may also feel better about herself if she identifies with the advocacy community, helping to bring positive change for human and nonhuman animals.

11

Misanthropy and Veganism

> **"** I don't care if what I say offends humans, because the animal holocaust is the worst atrocity this planet has ever seen! Screw humans and their feelings. I only care about the animals. **"**

We must guard against going down the dark road where we view all others as horrible and write off humans altogether. This is essentially the definition of a "misanthrope," which Merriam-Webster defines as "a person who hates or distrusts humankind." This is a topic that is also worth discussing apart from trauma, since misanthropy may not always result from trauma exposure, and some of the most prominent "leaders" in the movement are self-proclaimed misanthropes who regularly make statements such as the one in the text box above.

In chapter 10 I discussed how assuming the worst in others can lead to missed opportunities in recognizing openness to a vegan message. Beyond this problem, a misanthropic stance can contribute to the perception of the animal movement as exclusionary of those who are not able-bodied, cis-gendered whites. Insensitivity to others because "nonhuman animals have it the worst" does nothing to bring those from other social justice movements and marginalized communities into the animal movement.

In this sense, the animal advocacy movement is quite distinct from other social justice movements because the victims of the oppression are not actually participating in the advocacy.

Thus, there is greater opportunity for the loudest and most aggressive voices in the community to speak on behalf of those oppressed while others are further marginalized and distanced from the movement.

It should go without saying that there is no benefit to rank-ordering oppressions. There is nothing to be gained from attempting to determine which atrocity is the worst, or which form of oppression or injustice we will ignore. Of course, the more that we demonstrate insensitivity to others the less likely they will feel like they have a home within the movement.

Self-described misanthropic vegans often state that they should not need to modify their language to please others, that they will call things as they see them even if it means that it might be offensive to others. The problem with that mindset is that the language we use makes a big difference in helping others change. This is essentially what my profession as a psychologist is based on. If it didn't make a difference what words we said or the language that we used, there would be no point in making any efforts to help others change their behavior. There would be no such thing as animal advocacy either, unless it only involved direct rescue efforts. It makes no sense to engage in animal advocacy attempting to promote change in others while ignoring the obvious fact that words matter.

Those who describe themselves as misanthropic in their animal advocacy should be mindful of the impacts of their misanthropy and consider the function of their advocacy. For example, are they expressing anger and indifference toward other humans because it will somehow help nonhuman animals, or are they doing it to vent their own frustration at the horrors of the animal use industries' and others' indifference to them? This kind of self-examination can be helpful.

In my work in the area of violence prevention and anger management, I talk to my clients about how expressing anger is probably the easiest thing to do. It is much more challenging to convey the feelings beneath the anger and to communicate in ways that are compelling and influential. It is perhaps more work and more challenging to take a non-misanthropic stance, but I believe the difference it can make for the animals is well worth the effort.

12

Eating Disorders and Veganism

> Today my parents told me that I can't go vegan because they say that I have an eating disorder, which is ridiculous! They both come from farming families and say that veganism itself is an eating disorder. I have no concerns about my weight, I don't restrict my food intake, and don't binge or purse. I just want to stop contributing to animal cruelty.

I want to clear up some misconceptions about veganism and our connection with food. First, veganism is not a diet. It's a way of life that focuses on reducing the harm we do to nonhuman animals as much as we can. One way of doing this is by not eating them, but our dietary choice is just one aspect of a broader ethic to minimize harm to others.

Too often we see those who refer to themselves as vegans state that they need to set a "good example" and promote veganism by focusing on how their bodies look, which, again, is not the point of veganism. This is a harmful view on multiple levels because it can lead to fat shaming within the movement and causes others to feel alienated. This perspective also weakens the true ethical message underlying veganism.

There is no connection between wanting to minimize the harm we do to animals and having an eating disorder. In other words, going vegan for the animals does not place one at greater risk of developing an eating disorder. In fact, I believe that it's quite the opposite. I have heard so many vegans talk about how their veganism helped them recover from an eating disorder because it helped them focus on those other than themselves, and the feeling of reward and self-esteem they gained from trying to help animals helped them deal with their emotional issues.

Family members and loved ones would be wise to take caution about how they approach the young vegan in their lives. Immediately accusing her or him of having an eating disorder simply because they are vegan may serve to alienate them and may show a complete lack of understanding of their loved one, not to mention veganism and eating disorders in general. It is especially harmful to wrongfully suggest that a loved one has an eating disorder as a strategy to turn them away from veganism and in an attempt to control their behavior.

Can one who has an eating disorder choose a restrictive diet that excludes all animal sources of food? Yes, of course that can happen and it does happen, but that's not about veganism but rather the eating disorder. When one makes a sudden change to a plant-based diet and they have a history of eating disorder issues, it is understandable that their loved ones would want to ensure that this is not related to the eating disorder, and a visit with a nutritionist or other counselor may certainly be advisable. However, a balanced vegan diet is not harmful, and in fact can be extremely healthy, both physically and psychologically.

ANOREXIA AND VEGANISM

The following is written by Justin Van Kleeck, animal advocate and cofounder of "The Microsanctuary Movement," who himself struggled with an eating disorder and found his veganism to be helpful in his regaining his health and sense of well-being. This can also be found on the Vegan Publishers blog:[1]

What I remember most about my childhood years, especially my years in school, is feeling different because

I was overweight. The jokes and snide comments from my peers were, of course, the most obvious indicators that I was a bad person. But there were so many other, subtler signs that I am sure anyone in a similar position has felt.

This sort of awareness, at least for those who are sensitive to the attitudes and judgment of others, breeds a depressingly neurotic, obsessive self-criticism that often flowers into full-blown self-loathing.

And that was my mental and emotional state by high school. One of the clearest memories I have is of a period in which I would repeat, like a mantra, "I will get thin," as I lay in bed trying to go to sleep.

Admittedly, as a male who was both a good student and also a good athlete, living with my father in a single-parent household, it may seem strange that my weight was always and inevitably such an issue. But it was, and by age seventeen, I hated myself for it with every fiber of my being.

It was something of a miracle (to me), then, when my appetite suddenly disappeared during my junior year of high school. (The "miracle" was likely as much a psychological phenomenon as a physiological one.) I did not eat anything for several days, and afterward my entire relationship to food changed.

I realized for the first time that I could control both food and, more importantly (or so I thought), my body. I started eating strictly healthier foods, exercising a lot, and monitoring my weight.

I had topped out at 265 pounds. Eleven months later, when I came back from summer break for my senior year of high school, I was 135 pounds lighter. Friends I had known since middle school walked right by me in the hallway. Though I felt like absolute garbage—I could not walk up to the school's second story without losing my vision and needing to support myself for a moment to regain my senses—I had a rush of pride and satisfaction at having become, in a way, a new person.

My anorexia manifested as severe food restriction for a couple of years, allowing me to shake off weight like it was an oversized coat. After a hospitalization and extensive counseling, I managed to get away and go to college. My weight went up and down, but I eventually stopped seeing any counselors and was left to my own devices and disorders. I also went vegan at this time, after reading a pamphlet about animal agriculture (I had been vegetarian for two years before this point) and finally refusing to cause unnecessary suffering to other living beings through my diet and other choices. During my later years in college, I also lost more weight (though I was eating regularly), reaching a nadir of 114 pounds shortly before graduation.

A PhD program at a different university was a massive undertaking, but I managed to juggle depression, anorexia, and an extensive course load, as well as an unwavering commitment to veganism, for all of the five years it took me to finish. (A second hospitalization along the way was merely a speed bump.) It was habitual by that point, and I got so used to how my body felt while not eating enough that none of the minor issues fazed me. Indeed, feeling deprived and exhausted seemed justifiable to my self-loathing mind; I only got worried when I started to feel in any way good.

Things got genuinely scary for me only once. It was after graduate school, and I was working as a residential staff member at a massage therapy school in northern California during high-desert season. The climate was absolutely draining, and I could not stay nourished or hydrated enough to keep up. My condition deteriorated to the point that I could not walk up hills and I spent the weekends in a near-coma in my room.

It is a frightful thing to look in the mirror and see Death looking back at you—to see that it has taken over you, has become you.

I left California and returned to the East Coast to recuperate. I cannot say that the California experience changed things immediately, but I do believe it was a personal bottoming out that allowed me to slowly crawl back up to something resembling well-being.

There is no single thing I can point to as central to my ability to live with anorexia. (I do not say "recover" because it is always there. My relationships with food and my body are always tinged with the hues of anorexia, though it has become easier to not be blinded by them.) But I can say for certain that my ethical veganism was helpful in this growth.

Having rattled off that long, woeful narrative, I want to be crystal clear: *Veganism is not an eating disorder.*

My veganism was (and is) fully informed by a recognition that I am not the center of things, but only one small part. Veganism helped me to have something important to work on and be a part of through advocacy and activism. It was also crucial that I met another vegan who became my partner (and my wife), and that the two of us have undertaken so many projects on behalf of animals—be it caring for our big family of rescues, starting a sanctuary and education organization for farmed animals, or organizing events and classes to promote a vegan lifestyle. I have, finally, been able to focus on vastly more important things than myself and my neuroses by dedicating myself to an active, engaged life as a vegan.

Now, I look at the fifteen or so years that I was in the grip of my mind's stranglehold as an important part of my growth as a person. My eating disorder started before my veganism, but I know without question that the latter is not contingent upon the former. My veganism is a result of my inability to accept that others should needlessly suffer so that I might live. It has nothing to do with dieting, restricting food, or controlling how much I allow myself to eat.

My veganism is bigger and more central to who I am than my anorexia. I remember very clearly my process of going vegan, and there was not a single moment in which I considered being vegan because I could then restrict my food choices even more. Rather than veganism being a manifestation of a disorder, I am certain that veganism has been a crucial way for me to find balance and well-being in my own life while also motivating me to make a difference in the lives of others.

Thus, I cannot emphasize enough just how frustrating it is to me that mainstream media outlets frequently attempt to equate veganism with eating disorders. Making an ethical choice to remove oneself (as much as possible) from a system of needless suffering is not the same as restricting foods for health, calorie reduction, "right" eating, or even self-starvation. I dealt with this sort of reductive thinking about mental health and emotional issues from family and professionals alike, and it still raises my hackles to see the conflation of two causally unrelated things occur.

While I realize some people can and do stop eating animal products in order to restrict food, it is a grave error to turn those individual instances into indicators of the disordered heart of veganism as a whole. After all, how we interact with food is just one part of a vegan lifestyle. For me veganism is even more about having a larger perspective on how we impact other beings and the planet, grounded in the recognition that our wants, our issues, and our needs are all part of a vast ecosystem that is not centered on us.

13

Shopping Suggestions

> **"** When I first told my family that I was going vegan, they told me that I would have to buy my own food, when they knew that I had no money. So I would just eat whatever we had in the house: mostly pasta, rice, and oatmeal. I ended up feeling really sick. I was getting migraines and had zero energy. My family blamed it on my veganism, but I think it's just because my diet wasn't good. This morning, my mother told me that she's going to take me food shopping with her and that I can even pick out one of those vegan meat substitutes I have been hearing about! Do you have any advice? **"**

I often receive these kinds of messages from young vegans. It is sometimes a struggle to go vegan in a non-vegan home, especially if one is reliant on others to purchase the food. For some, this is an insurmountable problem, and many have told me that they plan on going vegan the moment they are old enough to move out and live on their own. I see this state of affairs as a real shame and something that can do lasting damage to relationships. For a family member or loved one to not allow a younger person to eat and otherwise live in a way that's consistent with their values, most likely because they hold false views about veganism or don't like to be reminded of their contribution to the harm of animals, is not conducive to a healthy relationship and can be damaging in a number of respects.

It is true that parents and caregivers who are purchasing the food have the right to decide what they will buy for their families, but if they have an interest in maintaining a positive and close relationship with their vegan loved one, attempting to put them in a situation where they feel forced to contribute to animal harm is simply not healthy.

My advice to younger vegans who are living with caregivers who refuse to buy vegan food is to be as open as they can with them about how this makes them feel, without blaming anyone and without anger or aggression. I suggest that they use plenty of "I statements" where they are focusing on their own feelings and not how others "make them feel." It is a lot harder for others to feel defensive when we are simply talking about how we feel. Sometimes family counseling can be very helpful in these situations if the communication is poor and only getting worse.

If the parent or caretaker still will not buy vegan food, the young vegan has to make a decision, and that decision may be based on the individual and the specifics of their situation.

For some, they feel like they simply can't go vegan in this environment and they often state that they will go vegetarian for now and vegan when they buy their own food. They typically recognize this is a far from ideal situation and it may cause them great distress and anxiety.

For others, they go forward with veganism, eating whatever vegan items are available in the household. Of course, "vegan food" is most food, aside from the flesh of a limited number of nonhuman animals and their secretions. Fruits, vegetables, nuts, seeds, and grains are all vegan and most people, even the most fervent meat eater, still consumes food that is not animal-based.

When I talk to a young vegan or aspiring vegan in this situation I approach them in a nonjudgmental way. There is no benefit for me showing disapproval when they're experiencing problems with their loved ones, feel unsupported, and may be having difficulties coping. Instead, I try to show understanding, and I support them on their desire to be vegan and their attempts at communicating why veganism is important to them.

In the case example above, however, the mother of the vegan agreed to do some shopping for vegan food. This can be a major breakthrough for this family and open the door to better communication and closeness. Making this gesture can demonstrate to the vegan loved one that their independence and strongly held convictions are valid and to be respected. When in this situation, I encourage the young vegan to be thankful and to show appreciation for this gesture. This is a major step!

Other young vegans need to figure out shopping when they leave the house for the first time to go to school or somewhere else. For many, this entails striving to find affordable, easy-to-prepare vegan foods that offer enough variety to ensure good nutrition.

So what should a young vegan look for when shopping? The best advice is to try to obtain a balanced diet that is high on whole foods and unprocessed foods, with plenty of fruits, vegetables, and legumes.

Some people prefer to make their initial vegan transition by eating a lot of replacement foods, which is a good strategy as well. There is a vegan alternative to any dish involving animal ingredients, and there are so many "transition foods" such as vegan meats that pretty much taste like the animal-based foods that people are accustomed to. However, the idea is to eventually transition to more of a whole foods diet and away from the processed foods.

It's also important to consider that the availability of healthy vegan food may vary widely depending on geographical locale. Some who live in "food deserts" and in rural areas with limited shopping options may have a more difficult time finding vegan options. Cost may also be a limiting factor, though in most places a vegan diet based that doesn't include more expensive vegan substitute products can be done affordably.

There are several tips here that may be useful for you before you go on your shopping trip.[1] First, it can be helpful to plan your menus to avoid wasting time and money. Choose recipes you will make and plan to buy all of the ingredients that you will need for the entire week. Make a list of all of the items and ingredients that you may need, and plan for food storage so that you don't waste any food. Gathering coupons can be one of the best strategies to save money when you shop. To prevent food spoilage, always buy your perishable items last and unpack them first when you get home. Harmful bacteria can increase substantially if the refrigerated food is left out too long and gets too warm.

I'm not a dietitian, but there are some well-known tips for healthy vegan eating that have helped me to improve my health and stay fit. I went from an unhealthy animal eater with an arthritic condition and immune system disorder to a completely healthy marathon runner within a year or two of going vegan. Results may vary, and not all vegan diets are necessarily healthy, but one can achieve several possible health benefits from a vegan diet.

First, and what I believe is most important, is to eat as many raw foods as possible, including fruits and vegetables, legumes, nuts, and seeds, and limit intake of oils, salt, and sugar. As long as you eat a variety of these foods, you should get enough protein and other nutrients, with the possible exception of B_{12} that may be supplemented. It's a good idea for everyone, vegan and non-vegan, to periodically have their levels checked via vitamin and nutrition blood tests.

There are a couple of resources that I think may be especially helpful in shopping vegan affordably. *In Pursuit of Great Food: A Plant-Based Shopping Guide*[2] covers all of the ins and outs of vegan shopping and what to look for and avoid. *Eat Vegan On $4 A Day*[3] is also a helpful cookbook that demonstrates how one can eat vegan using easy-to-find, affordable ingredients.

A valuable resource for those who drink wine, beer, and liquor is the website *Barnivore*, which allows one to search for different brands to determine whether or not they are vegan (yes, most wines are not vegan because animal ingredients are used in their production).

14

Coping with Anger

I saved this chapter for last because much of what I have covered thus far involves anger management, though not explicitly describing it as such, and there is value in tying it all together in one place. Millennials have a lot of reasons to be angry, and so do vegans, and thus millennial vegans could claim to be rightfully pissed off!

Seriously though, there is a lot of anger in the world right now, especially for young people who tend to be more "woke" than earlier generations and whose efforts are largely thwarted by bad decisions that they had nothing to do with. More and more, I am running across young people who feel that they need help managing their anger and other negative emotions.

I think it's important to point out that anger is not necessarily a bad thing, and nobody can take your anger away. Anger is a normal and natural emotion, it can alert us and others to real problems that we need to deal with, and it can help resolve problems if communicated effectively. In fact, as a therapist I am always more concerned about a patient who denies ever getting angry than a patient who describes frequent anger. A patient who denies anger is potentially dangerous because they are likely storing away their anger and denying its existence, rather than openly recognizing their feelings and dealing with them, which, as mentioned in chapter 3, is a recipe for an explosion.

I've run hundreds of anger management group sessions and have developed a violence prevention program that attempts to really get at the heart of the most important basic ingredients for managing anger and violence. In our programs, we hit on the following concepts and strategies again and again to make sure that our clients truly internalize them.

DEVELOP AWARENESS

Perhaps the most important element to managing one's anger is to become more aware of the components of their anger. The earlier we can recognize that our anger is starting to build, the better we can short-circuit that anger response and prevent things from going in the wrong direction. So many people have told me that they don't see their anger coming; they just explode into anger out of the blue. The truth is that this doesn't really happen. There is always a lead up to episodes of problematic anger expression, but most people just aren't aware of what's going on inside them.

The three main components to our anger that are important to be aware of are (1) our physiological responses, (2) our feelings, and (3) our thoughts.

Physiological responses often represent signs that one's "fight or flight" response is kicking in, such as experiencing an adrenaline rush, tightness in chest, clenched teeth, heart racing, turning red, shaking, and so on. These signs of tension and stress are warning signs for anger, and the more that we can do to counter such tension and stress, the less angry we will be. This is another reason why self-care and taking time to relax, have fun, and destress are so important; they help us to manage our anger.

Anger is perhaps the easiest emotion to identify and express. It can be easy to lash out at others, while it may be more challenging to recognize and express the "softer" feelings underlying that anger, such as sadness, disappointment, and anxiety. Identifying what's really underlying our anger can help us have greater awareness about why we are angry, and it can be an important early warning sign that our anger is escalating. Expressing those underlying feelings is also critical for managing anger. The more of the true feelings that we can recognize and express to

It is good to draft a written time-out plan to use with others. If you're in a relationship, it can be particularly helpful to develop a plan together with your partner. It's obviously best to draft this plan before any disagreement when both are calm, rather than negotiating terms in the heat of the moment. Here are some important elements to include:

- Who has the right to call a time-out? It should be either party.
- How do you call a time-out? Typically by letting the other person know you need to take a time-out, making a "time-out" hand signal, or by using a funny code word agreed upon by both parties beforehand. For obvious reasons, you never want to try to take a time-out by saying, "You need to take a time-out!"
- How long should the time-out last? Typically a half hour to an hour. If you need more time after that, just let the other person know that you need more time. It's best to avoid letting situations simmer and go without discussion overnight or for long periods of time.
- What do you do when a time-out has ended? Make sure that you discuss the issue that led to the time-out and express your true feelings below the anger.

Agreeing to a plan for cooling off during difficult situations may not always be possible, like when dealing with aggravating peers or coworkers, or even dealing with Internet trolls, but the same general principles apply. We can decide ahead of time that we will find a way to remove ourselves from situations that have a high potential for going badly so that we can better manage our anger and come back at a later time for discussion if we choose to do so.

Recently, many of the younger vegans that I know have been taking social media breaks or otherwise unplugging for periods of time to help manage anger and other negative emotions. This is also a good idea if it helps us cope better and puts us in a better mind space. As discussed in chapters 10 and 11, it's important that all of us are able to recognize when we are going to that dark place and do what we can to take care of ourselves. We do not do the animals any good if we are consumed by negative feelings like anger. An analogy to airline safety is sometimes used in animal advocacy circles: place the oxygen mask on ourselves first so we can better help others.

Communication Is Key

I have, at times, been complimented about how I'm able to keep my cool when dealing with Internet trolls and abusive behavior by others. My response is that I have had a lot of practice in my line of work. The truth is that in the past, I would have very aggressive responses when I perceived an attack because I had my own trauma issues to deal with and was not a good communicator. What I have learned is that when I communicate assertively and effectively, and consider why I feel the way that I do, I don't feel a need to lash out at anyone and I don't let things get to me nearly as much as I used to. Good communication is not only helpful in managing anger, but also a range of other problems, which makes sense since communication skills are taught to those in treatment for issues ranging from depression to eating disorders.

I have discussed and summarized many communication strategies throughout this book so I will not go into detail about all of them all here again, but here are some of the most fundamental communication points to take away:

- Develop a listening mindset and use active listening strategies, where you are showing the other person that you hear their perspective, even if you don't necessarily agree with it.
- Be assertive with others, rather than passive or aggressive.

- Express any angry feelings, but more importantly, express the feelings that underlie your anger.
- Do not engage in abusive behavior, and set firm limits for others' behavior so that you don't tolerate any abuse yourself.
- Don't assume you know what others are thinking and don't assume they know what you're thinking, because when we make assumptions, it's often in the negative direction and not accurate.
- Educate yourself about social justice issues so that you will feel less frustrated when communicating with others about them, and recognize your triggers and your limits when trying to help others change.
- Reach out to others when you need help or someone to communicate with, and communicate your needs to others.

I hope that you've found this book useful. For those of you who are struggling in different ways, may this book give you some comfort and provide you with some skills and tips for making it through. I can tell you that it will likely get better and better. I have met so many vegans who were on a rocky road at first, especially involving their relationships with others, but things improved greatly with time. So no matter how hard it gets, just understand that it's just a moment in time and that you have a lot of important work left to do.

Again, I am in awe of you and I am thankful for your ability to see through all of the conditioning in order to do the right thing for others. If this book gives you any strength to continue to advocate for animals, I am grateful. Please remember that our evolution is a lifelong process and you are still near the beginning of that process. You are not nearly done with your progression as a person and an advocate. We don't stop evolving once we become vegan. We keep growing and learning, and our veganism changes over time. Hopefully, we become more inclusive in our advocacy and become pro-intersectional in that we think of how different forms of oppression are linked and we fight against all injustice. Given the state of our world, getting at the roots of injustice is important work for us to take on.

I also hope that you keep in mind that working on relationships with family and other loved ones is, likewise, a lifelong process, and I hope that this book can serve as a resource to assist you with those relationships. Discussions around veganism and associated issues need not drive loved ones apart. Ideally, the more we are able to communicate about the things that matter to us, the closer we will be as families and as a society. Clear, honest, and respectful communication, with a lot of listening and the expression of feelings, is often a recipe for improved communication and closer relationships.

As with all things, however, there are no guarantees, and most of us will feel alone at times. During those times, we can take solace in the fact that we're serving a cause that's bigger than us. We're preventing needless suffering and death of others, which is about the most important work we can be doing. We should take pride in our efforts and feel good about ourselves. Yes, it's about the animals and not us, but doing the right thing by others is probably the best way to fight off our own depression and feelings of hopelessness. It gives greater meaning to our lives and a sense of purpose in a world that often seems cruel and senseless.

Someday we will have a vegan world. It may not be in our lifetime, but it will need to happen for us to remain on this planet. Until then, though, we have to take care of each other and build a supportive community. My door is always open to you, and if you ever need any advice, about advocacy or getting any other kind of help, please feel free to reach out to me. We will get through this together.

Notes

Preface: You Are Awesome

1. *Vegan Life Magazine.* (2016). "Veganism booms by 350%." www.vegan lifemag.com/veganism-booms.
2. Patten, E., & Fry, R. (2015, March). "How Millennials today compare with their grandparents 50 years ago." Pew Research Center.

Chapter 1: An Introduction to Veganism

1. The Vegan Society. (2014). "Ripened by human determination: 70 Years of The Vegan Society." www.vegansociety.com/sites/default/files/ uploads/ Ripened%20by%20human%20determination.pdf.
2. Yang, S. et al. (2012). "Chinese lacto-vegetarian diet exerts favorable effects on metabolic parameters, intima-media thickness, and cardiovascular risks in healthy men." *Nutrition in Clinical Practice.* 27.3. 392–398. The American Society for Parenteral and Enteral Nutrition.
3. Huang, T. et al. (2012). "Cardiovascular disease mortality and cancer incidence in vegetarians: a meta-analysis and systematic review." *Annals of Nutrition and Metabolism,* 60.4. 233–240.
4. Pettersen, B. et al. (2012). "Vegetarian diets and blood pressure among white subjects: Results from the Adventist Health Study-2 (AHS-2)." *Public Health Nutrition.* 15.10. 1909–1916.
5. Appleby, P., Allen, N., & Key, T. (2002). "Hypertension and blood pressure among meat eaters, fish eaters, vegetarians and vegans in EPIC-Oxford." *Public Health Nutrition.* 5.5. 645–654.
6. Huang, "Cardiovascular disease." Lanou, A. and B. Svenson. (2010). "Reduced cancer risk in vegetarians: An analysis of recent reports." *Cancer Management and Research.* 3. 1–8. 20.
7. Appleby, P., Allen, N., & Key, T. (2011). "Diet, vegetarianism, and cataract risk." *The American Journal of Clinical Nutrition.* 93.5. 1128–1135.
8. Giem, P., Beeson, W., & Fraser, G. (1992). "The incidence of dementia and intake of animal products: preliminary findings from the Adventist Health Study." *Neuroepidemiology.* 12.1. 28–36.

9. Gorczyca, D. et al. (2011). "An impact of the diet on serum fatty acid and lipid profiles in Polish vegetarian children and children with allergy." *European Journal of Clinical Nutrition*. 65. 191–195.

10. Melnik, B. (2012). "Dietary intervention in acne: Attenuation of increased mTORC1 signaling promoted by Western diet." *Dermato-Endocrinology*. 4.1. 20–32. 1.

11. Turner-McGrievy, G, N. Barnard, & A. Scialli. (2007). "A two-year randomized weight loss trial comparing a vegan diet to a more moderate low-fat diet." *Obesity*. 15.9. 2276–2281.

12. Barnard, N. et al. (2009). "A low-fat vegan diet and a conventional diabetes diet in the treatment of type 2 diabetes: A randomized, controlled, 74-week clinical trial." *The American Journal of Clinical Nutrition*. 89. 1588S–1596S.

13. Ornish, D. et al. (1998). "Intensive lifestyle changes for reversal of coronary heart disease." *The Journal of the American Medical Association*. 280.23. 2001–2007.

14. Ornish, D. et al. (2005). "Intensive lifestyle changes may affect the progression of prostate cancer." *Journal of Urology*. 174.3. 1065-1069.

15. FAO (2006). "Livestock a major threat to environment." *FAO Newsroom*. Rome: FAO, 26, www.fao.org/newsroom/en/news/2006/1000448/index.html.

16. Goodland, R., Anhang, J. (2009). "Livestock and climate change. What if the key actors in climate change are...pigs, cows and chickens?" *World Watch*. Nov/Dec 2009.

17. FAO, "Livestock."

18. Beckett, J., & Oltjen, J. (1993). "Estimation of the Water Requirement for Beef Production in the United States." *Journal of Animal Science*. 71. 818–8268.

19. Vidal, J. (2012). "Food shortages could force world into vegetarianism, warn scientists." *Ecologist*. 31 Aug. 2012.

20. USDA (2001). "Agricultural Statistics." Washington, D.C.: United States Department.

21. Steele, D. (2009). "Factory Farms' Wide Net of Pain and Destruction." *The Canada Earthsaver*.

22. EPA (2001, August). "Emissions From Animal Feeding Operations: Draft." xi. EPA,15. www.epa.gov/ttn/chief/ap42/ch09/draft/draftanimalfeed.pdf.

23. Boucher, D. et al. (2012). "Grade A Choice? Solutions for deforestation-free meat." Cambridge, MA: Union of Concerned Scientists.

24. Messina, V. and Mangels, R. (2001). "Considerations in planning vegan diets: children." *Journal of the American Dietetic Association*. 101. 661-669. Wasserman, D. & Mangels, R. (2006). Simply Vegan: Quick Vegetarian Meals. Baltimore, MD: The Vegetarian Resource Group.

25. Sellmeyer, D. et al. (2001). "A high ratio of dietary animal to vegetable protein increases the rate of bone loss and the risk of fracture in post-menopausal women." *American Journal of Clinical Nutrition*. 73. 118–22.

26. Knight, E., et al. (2003). "The impact of protein intake on renal function decline in women with normal renal function or mild insufficiency." *Annals of Internal Medicine*. 138. 460–7.

27. Lappe, F. (1971). Diet for a Small Planet. New York: Ballantine Books.

28. Gordon, D. (1996). "Vegetable Proteins Can Stand Alone." *Journal of the American Dietetic Association*. 96.3. 230-231. Lappe, F. (1981). *Diet for a Small Planet*. New York: Ballantine Books. Novick, J. (2003). "Complementary Protein Myth Won't Go Away!" *Healthy Times*. of Agriculture.

29. Norris, J., & Messina, V. (2011). *Vegan for Life*. Boston: Da Capo Press.

30. Gilsing, A., et al. (2010). "Serum concentrations of vitamin B12 and folate in British male omnivores, vegetarians and vegans: Results from a cross-sectional analysis of the EPIC-Oxford cohort study." *European Journal of Clinical Nutrition*. 64.9. 933–939. Grant, R. et al. (2008). "The relative impact of a vegetable-rich diet on key markers of health in a cohort of Australian adolescents." *Asia Pacific Journal of Clinical Nutrition*. 17.1. 107–115.

31. McDougall, J. (Nov. 2007) "Vitamin B12 Deficiency—the Meat-eaters' Last Stand." *The McDougall Newsletter*. 6.11.

32. Appold, K. (2012). "Dangers of Vitamin B12 Deficiency." *Aging Well*. 5.30.

33. Norris & Messina, *Vegan for Life*.

34. Schalinske, K. & Smazal, A. (Nov. 2012). "Homocysteine imbalance: A pathological metabolic marker." *Advances in Nutrition*. 3.6. 755–762.

35. Koebnick C. et al. (Dec. 2004). "Long-term ovo-lacto vegetarian diet impairs vitamin B-12 status in pregnant women." *Journal of Nutrition*. 134.12. 3319–26.

36. Baik, H., & Russell, R. (July, 1999). "Vitamin B12 deficiency in the elderly." *Annual Review of Nutrition*. 19. 357–377.

37. Norris & Messina, *Vegan for Life*.

38. *Will Travel for Vegan Food*, www.wtfveganfood.com.

39. Patrick-Goudreau, C. (2011). *Vegan's Daily Companion*.

40. Free From Harm. (2014). "Eating Animals: Addressing Our Most Common Justifications." http://freefromharm.org/eating-animals-addressing-our-most-common-justifications.

41. Sareen, A. (August 2012). "Why don't vegans care about people? *The Huffington Post*. http://m.huffpost.com/us/entry/1771404.

42. Ascione, F. (2005). Children and animals: Exploring the roots of kindness and cruelty [e-book]. West Lafayette, Ind: Purdue University Press; 2005.

43. Tallichet, S. (Autumn 2004). "Exploring the Link Between Recurrent Acts of Childhood and Adolescent Animal Cruelty and Subsequent Violent Crime." *Criminal Justice Review*. 29. 304–316.

44. Eisnitz, G. (2006). Slaughterhouse: *The Shocking Story of Greed, Neglect, and Inhumane Treatment Inside the U.S. Meat Industry*. Amherst, NY: Prometheus Books.

45. The Curvy Vegan (2014). "Angela Davis: Why Being Vegan is a Part of a Revolutionary Perspective." www.thecurvyvegan.com/angela-davis-vegan.html. Tuttle, W. (Ed.). (2014). *Circles of Compassion: Connecting Issues of Justice*. Vegan Publishers.

46. Crenshaw, K. (1991). "Mapping the margins: Intersectionality, Identity Politics, and Violence against Women of Color." *Stanford Law Review* 43(6):1241–1299. Knudsen, S. V. (2006). "Intersectionality – A Theoretical Inspiration in the Analysis of Minority Cultures and Identities in Textbooks" 61–76 in E. Bruillard, B. Aamotsbakken, S., Knudsen, S.

47. Jones, P. (October 11, 2013). "Intersectionality and Animals." *Vine Sanctuary News*.

48. Mills, M. "The Comparative Anatomy Of Eating." *Vegsource.com*. VegSource Interactive, Inc., 21 Nov. 2009. Web.

49. Hart, D., & Sussman, R. (2005). *Man the Hunted: Primates, Predators, and Human Evolution*. Cambridge, MA: Westview Press.

50. Jaffe Jones, E. (2011). *Eat Vegan on $4 a Day: A Game Plan for the Budget Conscious Cook*. Summertown, TN: Book Publishing Company.

Chapter 3: Assertive Vegan Communication

1. Taft, C. (2016). *Motivational Methods for Vegan Advocacy*. Danvers, MA: Vegan Publishers.

2. Krupnick, J. L., Sotsky, S. M., Simmens, S., Moyer, J., Elkin, I., Watkins, J., & Pilkonis, P. A. (1996). "The role of the therapeutic alliance in psychotherapy and pharmacotherapy outcome: Findings in the National Institute of Mental Health Treatment of Depression Collaborative Research Program." *Journal of Consulting and Clinical Psychology*, 64, 532–539.

Chapter 4: Psychological Abuse and Bullying

1. Breiding, M.J., Chen J., & Black, M.C. (2014). "Intimate Partner Violence in the United States — 2010." Atlanta, GA: National Center for Injury Prevention and Control, Centers for Disease Control and Prevention.

Chapter 5: Tips for Communicating with Others about Veganism

1. Free From Harm.

Chapter 6: Challenges Communicating with Loved Ones

1. Taft, *Motivational Methods*.
2. Christensen, A., & Jacobson, N. S. (1998). *Acceptance and Change in Couple Therapy: A Therapist's Guide to Transforming Relationships*. W.W. Norton and Company (1st edition).

Chapter 8: Masculinity, Sex, and Veganism

1. Rozin, P. et al. "Is Meat Male? A Quantitative Multimethod Framework to Establish Metaphoric Relationships." *Journal of Consumer Research*. 39.3. 629-643. The University of Chicago Press, 2012.
2. Norris & Messina, Vegan for Life.
3. Messina, M. (May 2010). "Soybean isoflavone exposure does not have feminizing effects on men: A critical examination of the clinical evidence." *Fertility and Sterility*. 93.7. 2095-2104.
4. Hamilton-Reeves, J. et al. (Aug. 2010). "Clinical studies show no effects of soy protein or isoflavones on reproductive hormones in men: results of a meta-analysis." *Fertility and Sterility*. 94. 997–1007.
5. Chavarro, J. et al. (Nov. 2008). "Soy food and isoflavone intake in relation to semen quality parameters among men from an infertility clinic." *Human Reproduction*. 23. 2584–2590.
6. Sharp, A. (2015). "Horny Herbivore or Flaccid Flower: Does Going Vegan Increase Your Libido?" veganmotivation.com/does-going-vegan-increase-your-libido.
7. Beezhold, B. L., & Johnston, C. S. (2012). Restriction of meat, fish, and poultry in omnivores improves mood: A pilot randomized controlled trial. *Nutrition Journal*, 11:9.

Chapter 10: Trauma in Animal Advocacy

1. Adams, C. (1990). *The Sexual Politics of Meat: A Feminist Vegetarian Critical Theory*. Continuum International Publishing Group.

Chapter 12: Eating Disorders and Veganism

1. Van Kleeck, Justi.n (2014). "Anorexia and Veganism: My Story," http://veganpublishers.com/anorexia-and-veganism-my-story-justin-van-kleeck.

Chapter 13: Shopping Suggestions

1. Strombom, A., & Rose, S. (2015). *In Pursuit of Great Food: A Plant-Based Shopping Guide*. Danvers, MA: Vegan Publishers.
2. Ibid.
3. Jaffe Jones. *Eat Vegan on $4 a Day*.

About the Author

Casey T. Taft, PhD, is a psychologist and Professor of Psychiatry at Boston University School of Medicine. He is an internationally recognized clinical researcher in the area of family violence prevention and the winner of prestigious awards for his work from the International Society for Traumatic Stress Studies; the Institute on Violence, Abuse, and Trauma; and the Centers for Disease Control and Prevention.

Dr. Taft has served as Principal Investigator on funded grants focusing on understanding and preventing partner violence through the National Institute of Mental Health, the Department of Veterans Affairs, the Centers for Disease Control, the Department of Defense, the Blue Shield Foundation of California, and the Bob Woodruff Foundation. He was the primary developer of the Strength at Home programs, which were the first and only programs shown to prevent and end family violence in military populations through randomized controlled trials. He is currently funded to implement these programs across healthcare systems and within military settings.

Dr. Taft is on the Editorial Boards of five journals. He has chaired an American Psychological Association task force on trauma in the military and the American Psychological Association has recently published his book, *Trauma-Informed Treatment and Prevention of Intimate Partner Violence*. He has also consulted with the United Nations on preventing violence and abuse globally, and is president of the board of directors for the Common Purpose intimate partner violence intervention program.

Dr. Taft is a dedicated vegan and views his veganism as an extension of his violence prevention work. Cofounder of Vegan Publishers, his goal is to raise vegan awareness and address the roots of violence and trauma. Author of *Motivational Methods for Vegan Advocacy: A Clinical Psychology Perspective*, Dr. Taft is an expert in applying theories and practices of clinical psychology to the animal advocacy realm.